Knit Your Own
BROONS®

JACKIE HOLT & RUTH BAILEY

BLACK & WHITE PUBLISHING

First published 2014
by Black & White Publishing Ltd
29 Ocean Drive, Edinburgh EH6 6JL

1 3 5 7 9 10 8 6 4 2   14 15 16 17

ISBN: 978 1 910230 04 6

LOTTERY FUNDED

A CIP catalogue record for this book is available
from the British Library.

Design by Stuart Polson Design
Printed and bound in the EU

Contents

Scotland's Favourite Family!

From the first publication in March 1936, the Broons have appeared every week in the *Sunday Post*'s Fun Section. The characters have changed slightly throughout the years, but they have never aged. Generations have followed the ploys of the characters who have become household names and are Scotland's best-loved folk.

Artist Dudley D. Watkins was first employed by DC Thomson in 1925. He worked on various kinds of illustrations but had a special gift for cartoons. He drew wonderful strips for *The Beano*, *The Dandy*, *The Beezer* and *The Topper*, as well as *The Broons* and *Oor Wullie*. His detailed and genuinely funny artwork is still enjoyed by readers today.

Watkins died in 1969, but the Broon family have continued to entertain us thanks to Tom Lavery, Ken H. Harrison and current artist Peter Davidson. For over seventy-five years, Maw, Paw, Granpaw, Joe, Hen, Maggie, Daphne, Horace, the Twins and the Bairn have been making us laugh with their mix-ups, misunderstandings, fallouts and family fun.

For us, *Knit Your Own Broons* is a celebration of these fantastic comics and a great way to reminisce on our childhood. It's a lot of fun and a great way to introduce your children, nieces, nephews and grandchildren (and maybe a few oldies!) to the ageless quality of this famous family's stories.

Jackie & Ruth ✗

PS: We've done our very best to make sure the patterns work perfectly, but please do check the website www.knityourownbroons.co.uk for updates and minor amends or additional explanations. Enjoy!

Paw's gone fishin' again!

You will need

MATERIALS:

Colour Codes:
1 Rowan Baby Merino Silk DK
(Shade SH674 – Shell Pink) – For Body
2 Debbie Bliss Rialto 4ply
(Shade 22003 – Black) – For Boots
3 Sublime Lace (Shade 0398 – Charcoal) –
For Suit (Knitted together with 4) and Hair
4 Rowan Fine Lace (Shade 00929 – Charcoal –
For suit (Knitted together with 3)
5 Anchor Artiste Baby Soft
(Shade 0403 – Black) – For Waistcoat back
6 Debbie Bliss Rialto Lace
(Shade 44002 – Pale Grey) – Shirt
7 Rowan Fine Tweed
(Shade Pendle 377 – Charcoal) – For Cap
8 Milla Mia Naturally Soft Merino
(Shade Cobalt 180 – Blue) – For Tie
9 Debbie Bliss Andes
(Shade 370019 – Pale Grey) – Whiskers

Beads for jacket buttons, waistcoat and eyes
Small white beads for shirt cuffs
Yarn for creating facial features and
stripes on tie
Reel of grey thread
Stuffing

NEEDLES:

Size 10/3.25mm
Size 12/2.75mm
Size 12/2.75mm double-ended
Size 14/2mm
Size 14/2mm double-ended
Crochet hook 3.5mm
Darning needle

Paw

Paw Broon has worn the same suit since 1936.
He drinks his tea out of the same saucer too. He has
rarely been seen to do the housework unless forced
to (or if Maw punishes him for misbehaving).
An affectionate and well-meaning father and husband,
he and his own father, the legendary Granpaw Broon,
can get into worse trouble than the bairns!

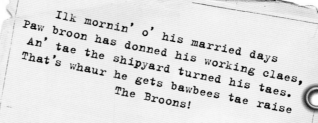

24

Ilk mornin' o' his married days
Paw broon has donned his working claes,
An' tae the shipyard turned his taes.
That's whaur he gets bawbees tae raise
The Broons!

BODY

COLOUR I
- Size 10/3.25mm needles

BODY – FRONT
- Cast on 16
- 1st row: K
- 2nd row: P
- 3rd row: K1, inc in next, K12, inc in next, K1 (18sts)
- Work 3 rows SS, starting with P
- 7th row: K1, K2tog, K2, K2tog, K4, K2tog, K2, K2tog, K1 (14sts)
- Work 3 rows SS, starting with P
- 11th row: K2, inc in next, K8, inc in next, K2 (16sts)
- 12th row: P
- 13th row: Inc in 1st, K3, inc in next, K6, inc in next, K3, inc in last (20sts)
- Work 7 rows SS, starting with P
- 21st row: K1, K2tog, K14, K2tog, K1 (18sts)
- Work 3 rows SS, starting with P
- 25th row: K1, sl1, K1, psso, K12, K2tog, K1 (16sts)
- 26th row: P1, P2tog, P10, P2tog, P1 (14sts)
- 27th row: K1, sl1, K1, psso, K8, K2tog, K1 (12sts)
- 28th row: P
- Cast off

BODY – BACK
COLOUR I
- Cast on 16
- 1st row: K
- 2nd row: P
- 3rd row: K2, inc in next, K1, inc in next, K6, inc in next, K1, inc in next, K2 (20sts)
- 4th row: P

- 5th row: K3, inc in next, K1, inc in next, K8, inc in next, K1, inc in next, K3 (24sts)
- Work 3 rows SS, starting with P
- 9th row: K1, K2tog, K18, K2tog, K1 (22sts)
- 10th row: P
- 11th row: K2, K2tog, K1, K2tog, K8, K2tog, K1, K2tog, K2 (18sts)
- 12th row: P
- 13th row: (K2, K2tog)x4, K2 (14sts)
- Work 5 rows SS, starting with P
- 19th row: K1, inc in next, K4, inc in next, inc in next, K4, inc in next, K1 (18sts)
- Work 9 rows SS beginning with P
- 29th row: K1, sl1, K1, psso, K12, K2tog, K1 (16sts)
- 30th row: P1, P2tog, P10, P2tog, P1 (14sts)
- 31st row: K1, sl1, K1, psso, K8, K2tog, K1 (12sts)
- 32nd row: P
- Cast off

To make up: Join front to back. Stuff.

ARMS – MAKE TWO

COLOUR I
- Size 10/3.25mm needles

WORKING FROM SHOULDER TO WRIST
- Cast on 5
- 1st row: K
- 2nd row: P
- 3rd row K1, inc in next, K1, inc in next, K1 (7sts)
- 4th row: P
- 5th row: K1, inc in next, K3, inc in next, K1 (9sts)
- 6th row: P
- 7th row: K3, inc in next, K1, inc in next, K3 (11sts)

- 8th row: P
- 9th row: K5, inc in next, K5 (12sts)
- Work 8 rows SS, starting with P
- 18th row: P2tog, P3, P2tog, P3, P2tog (9sts)
- 19th row: K2tog, K5, K2tog (7sts)
- 20th row: P
- 21st row: K1, inc in next, K3, inc in next, K1 (9sts)
- 22nd row: P
- 23rd row: K3, inc in next, K1, inc in next, K3 (11sts)
- Work 4 rows SS, starting with P
- 28th row: P1, P2tog, P5, P2tog, P1 (9sts)
- 29th row: K
- 30th row: P1, P2tog, P3, P2tog, P1 (7sts)
- 31st row: K
- 32nd row: P1, P2tog, P1, P2tog, P1 (5sts)
- 33rd row: K1, inc in next, K1, inc in next, K1 (7sts)
- 34th row: P
- 35th row: K1, inc in next, K3, inc in next, K1 (9sts)
- 36th row: P

FOR LEFT HAND
- 37th row: K2, put 2sts on pin, K5 (7sts)
- Work 4 rows SS, starting with P
- 42nd row: P2tog, P2tog, P2tog, P1 (4sts)
- 43rd row: K2tog, K2tog (2sts)
- Pull wool through

FOR RIGHT HAND
- 37th row: K5, put 2sts on pin, K2 (7sts)
- Work 4 rows SS, starting with P
- 42nd row: P1, P2tog, P2tog, P2tog (4sts)
- 43rd row: K2tog, K2tog (2sts)
- Pull wool through

THUMB – SAME FOR BOTH HANDS

- Join wool to 2sts on pin
- Use 12/2.75mm double-ended needles to work i-cord for 3 rows
- Pull wool through and darn end

To make up: Join seams. Stuff

BOOTS AND LEGS – MAKE TWO

COLOUR 2

- Size 10/3.25mm needles

- Cast on 20
- 1st row: K
- 2nd row: P
- 3rd row: K8, K2tog, K2tog, K8 (18sts)
- 4th row: P8, P2tog, P8 (17sts)
- 5th row: K
- 6th row: P
- 7th row: K4, cast off 9, K3 (8sts)
- 8th row: P, pulling 2 sections of 4sts together
- Work 4 rows SS, starting with K
- 13th row: K1, inc in next, K4, inc in next, K1 (10sts)
- 14th row: P
- Break wool, JOIN COLOUR 1
- Work 6 rows SS, starting with K
- 21st row: K1, inc in next, K6, inc in next, K1 (12sts)
- Work 24 rows SS, starting with P
- Cast off

To make up: Sew-up sole of boot – stuff boot. Join leg seam and stuff.

Tip: Stuff boots with offcuts of black wool

rather than white wadding, which tends to show through.

HEAD

COLOUR 1

- Size 10/3.25mm needles

HEAD – BACK

- Cast on 6
- 1st row: K
- 2nd row: P
- 3rd row: K
- 4th row: P, inc in 1st and last (8sts)
- Work 2 rows SS, starting with K
- 7th row: K row, inc in 1st and last (10sts)
- 8th row: P
- 9th row: K3, inc in next, K2, inc in next, K3 (12sts)
- 10th row: P
- 11th row: K2, (inc in next)x3, K2, (inc in next)x3, K2 (18sts)
- Work 5 rows SS, starting with P
- 17th row: K1, sl1, K1, psso, K2, sl1, K1, psso, K4, K2tog, K2, K2tog, K1 (14sts)
- 18th row: P
- 19th row: K1, (sl1, K1, psso)x3, (K2tog)x3, K1 (8sts)
- 20th row: P
- Cast off

HEAD – FRONT (RIGHT SIDE)

- Cast on 5
- 1st row: K
- 2nd row: P
- 3rd row: Cast on 2, K to end (7sts)
- 4th row: P5, inc in next, inc in next (9sts)
- 5th row: K1, inc in next, inc in next, K6 (11sts)

- 6th row: P11 – break wool, leave sts on needle

HEAD – FRONT (LEFT SIDE)

- With WS facing cast on 5, turn – now working on these 5sts only:
- 1st row: K
- 2nd row: P
- 3rd row: K, cast on 2 (7sts)
- 4th row: P1, inc in next, inc in next, P4 (9sts)
- 5th row: K6, inc in next, inc in next, K1 (11sts)
- 6th row: P11
- 7th row: K across 2 pieces to join, K10, K2tog, K10 (21sts)
- 8th row: P1, P2tog, P15, P2tog, P1 (19sts)
- Work 4 rows SS, starting with K
- 13th row: K1, sl1, K1, psso, K13, K2tog, K1 (17sts)
- 14th row: P
- 15th row: K1, sl1, K1, psso, K11, K2tog, K1 (15sts)
- 16th row: P
- 17th row: K1, sl1, K1, psso, K9, K2tog, K1 (13sts)
- 18th row: P1, P2tog, P7, P2tog, P1 (11sts)
- 19th row: K1, sl1, K1, psso, K5, K2tog, K1 (9sts)
- 20th row: P
- Cast off

To make up: Join seam under chin. Join front and back tog. Stuff. Attach to body.

SHIRT

COLOUR 6

- Size 14/2mm needles
- Size 14/2mm double-ended needles

MAIN BODY OF SHIRT
- Cast on 66
- 1st row: K
- 2nd row: K2, P62, K2
- Repeat rows 1 and 2 (x10)
- 23rd row: K17, cast off 2, K27, cast off 2, K16 (62sts)

FRONT LEFT SIDE – WITH WS FACING
- Working on 17sts – Put remaining sts on pin
- Work 14 rows SS, starting with P – Each P row starting with K2
- 15th row: Cast off 3, P to end (14sts)
- 16th row: K
- 17th row: Cast off 2, P to end (12sts)
- 18th row: Cast off 5, K to end (7sts)
- 19th row: P
- Cast off 7
- Pull wool through

SHIRT – BACK – WITH WS FACING – WORKING ON NEXT 28STS FROM PIN
- Work 16 rows SS, starting with P
- 17th row: Cast off 11, P16 (17sts)
- 18th row: Cast off 11 and leave remaining 6sts on pin for collar.

FRONT RIGHT SIDE – WITH WS FACING
- Working on remaining 17sts
- Work 13 rows SS, starting with P – Each P row ending with K2
- 14th row: Cast off 3, K to end (14sts)
- 15th row: P all sts
- 16th row: Cast off 2, K to end (12sts)
- 17th row: Cast off 5, P to end (7sts)
- 18th row: K
- Cast off

Join shoulder seams.

COLLAR – WITH RS FACING
- Pick up 11 sts along right front neck, K6 from pin across back neck, pick up 11 sts along left front neck (28sts), turn –

WITH WS FACING
- 1st row: K
- 2nd row: K1, P26, K1
- 3rd row: K
- 4th row: K1, P26, K1
- 5th row: K1, inc in next, K5, inc in next, K1, inc in next, K8, inc in next, K1, inc in next, K5, inc in next, K1 (34sts)
- 6th row: K1, P32, K1
- 7th row: K
- 8th row: K1, P32, K1
- 9th row: K33, inc in last (35sts)
- Cast off

SLEEVES
LEFT SLEEVE – WORKING FROM SHOULDER TO WRIST
- Cast on 32
- Work 9 rows SS, starting with K
- 10th row: P1, P2tog, P26, P2tog, P1 (30sts)
- Work 9 rows SS, starting with K
- 20th row: P1, P2tog, P24, P2tog, P1 (28sts)
- Work 9 rows SS, starting with K
- 30th row: P1, P2tog, P22, P2tog, P1 (26sts)
- Work 9 rows SS, starting with K
- 40th row: P1, P2tog, P20, P2tog, P1 (24sts)
- 41st row: K this row onto 3 double-ended needles
- 42nd row: P6, turn –
- 43rd row: K6, K18 from other end of needles (this closes the underarm seam and gives a vent opening at the side back), turn –
- 44th row: P

- 45th row: K
- 46th row: P
- 47th row: K3, (K2tog, K2) x2, K2tog, K1, (K2tog) x4, K2 (17sts)
- 48th row: K17, cast on 3 (20sts) – this makes the cuff in reverse SS
- 49th row: K1, P18, K1
- 50th row: K
- 51st row: K1, P18, K1
- 52nd row: K
- Cast off

RIGHT SLEEVE – WORKING FROM SHOULDER TO WRIST
- Cast on 32
- Work 9 rows SS, starting with K
- 10th row: P1, P2tog, P26, P2tog, P1 (30sts)
- Work 9 rows SS, starting with K
- 20th row: P1, P2tog, P24, P2tog, P1 (28sts)
- Work 9 rows SS, starting with K
- 30th row: P1, P2tog, P22, P2tog, P1 (26sts)
- Work 9 rows SS, starting with K
- 40th row: P1, P2tog, P20, P2tog, P1 (24sts)
- 41st row: K this row onto 3 double-ended needles
- 42nd row: P18, turn –
- 43rd row: K18, K6 from other end of needles (this closes the underarm seam and gives a vent opening at the side back), turn –
- 44th row: P
- 45th row: K
- 46th row: P
- 47th row: K2, (K2tog) x4, K1, K2tog, (K2, K2tog) x2, K3 (17sts)
- 48th row: Cast on 3, knit to end (20sts) – this makes the cuff in reverse SS
- 49th row: K1, P18, K1
- 50th row: K

- 51st row: K1, P18, K1
- 52nd row: K
- Cast off

To make up: Sew up sleeve seams and inset sleeves. Dress doll and stitch front together with COLOUR 6. Roll up sleeves to just above elbow. Catch with a stitch.

TROUSERS

COLOURS 3 AND 4 KNITTED TOGETHER
- Size 12/2.75mm needles

RIGHT LEG
- Cast on 21
- Work 20 rows SS, starting with K
- 21st row: K19, inc in next, K1 (22sts)
- Work 5 rows SS, starting with P
- 27th row: K1, inc in next, K18, inc in next, K1 (24sts)
- Work 7 rows SS, starting with P
- 35th row: K1, inc in next, K20, inc in next, K1 (26sts)
- Work 7 rows SS, starting with P
- 43rd row: K1, inc in next, K11, inc in next, K10, inc in next, K1 (29sts)
- Work 5 rows SS, starting with P
- 49th row: K1, inc in next, K25, inc in next, K1 (31sts)
- 50th row: P
- 51st row: K15, inc in next, K15 (32sts)
- Work 3 rows SS, starting with P
- 55th row: K16, inc in next, K15 (33sts)
- Work 3 rows SS, starting with P
- 59th row: K1, inc in next, K14, inc in next, K14, inc in next, K1 (36sts)
- 60th row: P
- 61st row: Cast off 2, K to end (34sts)

- 62nd row: Cast off 3, P to end (31sts)
- 63rd row: K
- 64th row: P2tog, P to end (30sts)
- Hold on a pin

LEFT LEG
- Cast on 21
- Work 20 rows SS, starting with K
- 21st row: K1, inc in next, K19 (22sts)
- Work 5 rows SS, starting with P
- 27th row: K1, inc in next, K18, inc in next, K1 (24sts)
- Work 7 rows SS, starting with P
- 35th row: K1, inc in next, K20, inc in next, K1 (26sts)
- Work 7 rows SS, starting with P
- 43rd row: K1, inc in next, K10, inc in next, K11, inc in next, K1 (29sts)
- Work 5 rows SS, starting with P
- 49th row: K1, inc in next, K25, inc in next, K1 (31sts)
- 50th row: P
- 51st row: K15, inc in next, K15 (32sts)
- Work 3 rows SS, starting with P
- 55th row: K15, inc in next, K16 (33sts)
- Work 3 rows SS, starting with P
- 59th row: K1, inc in next, K14, inc in next, K14, inc in next, K1 (36sts)
- 60th row: P
- 61st row: Cast off 3, K to end (33sts)
- 62nd row: Cast off 2, P to end (31sts)
- 63rd row: K
- 64th row: P29, P2tog (30sts)

KNITTING LEGS TOGETHER, STARTING WITH LEFT LEG
- 65th row: K28, K last stitch of left leg with first stitch of right leg together, K28 (57sts)

- Work 4 rows SS, starting with P
- 70th row: P2tog, P53, P2tog (55sts)
- Work 6 rows SS, starting with K
- 77th row: K18, K2tog, K15, K2tog, K18 (53sts)
- Work 4 rows starting with P
- Cast off

To make up: Join inside leg seams. Join crotch. Dress doll.

WAISTCOAT
COLOURS 3 AND 4 KNITTED TOGETHER
- Size 12/2.75mm needles

RIGHT FRONT
- Cast on 16
- 1st row: K11, turn –
- 2nd row: P10, K1
- 3rd row: K16
- 4th row: P15, K1
- 5th row: K
- 6th row: P15, K1
- 7th row: K
- 8th row: P15, K1
- 9th row: K
- 10th row: P15, K1
- 11th row: K14, inc in next, K1 (17sts)
- 12th row: P16, K1
- 13th row: K
- 14th row: P16, K1
- 15th row: K
- 16th row: P16, K1
- 17th row: K
- 18th row: P16, K1
- 19th row: K
- 20th row: Cast off 3, P12, K1 (14sts)
- 21st row: K12, K2tog (13sts)
- 22nd row: K2tog, p10, K1 (12sts)
- 23rd row: K1, sl1, K1, psso, K to end (11sts)
- 24th row: K1, P9, K1 (7sts)
- 25th row: K1, sl1, K1, psso, K to end (10sts)
- 26th row: K1, P8, K1
- 27th row: K1, sl1, K1, psso, K to end (9sts)
- 28th row: K1, P7, K1
- 29th row: K1, sl1, K1, psso, K to end (8sts)
- 30th row: K1, P6, K1
- 31st row: K1, sl1, K1, psso, K to end (7sts)
- 32nd row: K1, P5, K1
- 33rd row: K1, sl1, K1, psso, K to end (6sts)
- 34th row: K1, P2, P2tog, K1 (5sts)
- 35th row: K
- Cast off

LEFT FRONT
- Cast on 16
- 1st row: K1, P10, turn –
- 2nd row: K11
- 3rd row: K1, P to end
- 4th row: K
- 5th row: K1, P to end
- 6th row: K
- 7th row: K1, P to end
- 8th row: K
- 9th row: K1, P to end
- 10th row: K
- 11th row: K1, P to end
- 12th row: K1, inc in next, K14 (17sts)
- 13th row: K1, P to end
- 14th row: K
- 15th row: K1, P to end
- 16th row: K
- 17th row: K1, P to end
- 18th row: K
- 19th row: K1, P to end
- 20th row: Cast off 3, K to end (14sts)
- 21st row: K1, P11, P2tog (13sts)
- 22nd row: K2tog, K to end (12sts)
- 23rd row: K1, P2tog, P8, K1 (11sts)
- 24th row: K
- 25th row: K1, P2tog, p7, K1 (10sts)
- 26th row: K
- 27th row: K1, P2tog, P6, K1 (9sts)
- 28th row: K
- 29th row: K1, P2tog, P5, K1 (8sts)
- 30th row: K
- 31st row: K1, P2tog, P4, K1 (7sts)
- 32nd row: K
- 33rd row: K1, P2tog, P3, K1 (6sts)
- 34th row: K3, K2tog, K1 (5sts)
- Cast off

BACK
COLOUR 5
- Size 14/2mm needles

- Cast on 24
- Work 6 rows SS, starting with K
- 7th row: K1, K2tog, K8, K2tog, K8, K2tog, K1 (21sts)
- Work 3 rows SS, starting with P
- 11th row: K10, inc in next, K10 (22sts)
- 12th row: P
- 13th row: K10, inc in next, inc in next, K10 (24sts)
- Work 4 rows SS, starting with P
- 18th row: Cast off 2, P to end (22sts)
- 19th row: Cast off 2, K to end (20sts)
- 20th row: P2tog, P16, P2tog (18sts)
- Work 9 rows SS, starting with K
- 30th row: P6, turn –
- 31st row: K6
- 32nd row: P5, turn –
- 33rd row: K5
- 34th row: Cast off 5, P to end (13sts)
- 35th row: K6, turn –
- 36th row: P6
- 37th row: K5, turn –
- 38th row: P5
- Cast off all sts

To make up: Join front to back at side seams and shoulder seams. Dress doll. Close front and add beads for buttons.

JACKET

COLOURS 3 AND 4
- Size 12/2.75mm needles

FRONT AND BACK – LEFT
- Cast on 30
- 1st row: K
- 2nd row: K1, P28, K1
- Repeat rows 1 and 2 ten more times
- 13th row: K14, K2tog, K14 (29sts)
- 14th row: K1, P27, K1
- Set aside on a pin

FRONT AND BACK – RIGHT
- Cast on 33
- 1st row: K
- 2nd row: K1, P31, K1
- Repeat rows 1 and 2 10 more times
- 13th row: K14, K2tog, K17 (32sts)
- 14th row: Cast off 3, P27, K1 (29sts)

TO JOIN JACKET PIECES TOGETHER
- With RS facing work row 15 across front and back right, followed by front and back left
- 15th row: K28, K last stitch from right side and first from left side together, K28 (57sts)
- 16th row: K1, P55, K1
- 17th row: K
- 18th row: K1, P55, K1
- 19th row: K17, K2tog, K19, K2tog, K17 (55sts)
- 20th row: K1, P53, K1
- 21st row: K
- 22nd row: K1, P53, K1
- 23rd row: K17, inc in next, K19, inc in next, K17 (57sts)
- 24th row: K1, P55, K1
- 25th row: K15, inc in next, K25, inc in next, K15 (59sts)
- 26th row: K1, P57, K1
- 27th row: K
- 28th row: K1, P57, K1
- 29th row: K1, inc in next, K55, inc in next, K1 (61sts)
- 30th row: K2, P57, K2
- 31st row: K1, P2, K55, P2, K1
- 32nd row: K4, P13, cast off 3, P20, cast off 3, P12, K4 (55sts)

WORKING ON RIGHT FRONT (17STS)
- 33rd row: K1, P3, K13
- 34th row: P2tog, P11, K4 (16sts)
- 35th row: K1, P3, K12
- 36th row: P2tog, P9, K5 (15sts)
- 37th row: K1, P4, K10
- 38th row: P10, K5
- 39th row: K1, P5, K7, K2tog (14sts)
- 40th row: P8, K6
- 41st row: K1, P5, K8
- 42nd row: P7, K7
- 43rd row: K1, P6, K7
- 44th row: P7, K7
- 45th row: Cast off 4, P2, K7 (10sts)
- 46th row: P7, put last 3 sts onto pin for collar, turn –
- 47th row: K7
- 48th row: Cast off 3, P3 (4sts)
- Cast off

WORKING ON JACKET BACK – NEXT 21 STS – RS FACING
- Work 9 rows SS, starting with K
- 42nd row: P2tog, P17, P2tog (19sts)
- Work 4 rows SS, starting with K
- 47th row: Cast off 3, K15 (16sts)
- 48th row: Cast off 3, P12 (13sts)
- 49th row: Cast off 2, K10 (11sts)
- 50th row: Cast off 2, put remaining 9 sts on pin for collar

WORKING ON FRONT LEFT – REMAINING 17 STS – RS FACING
- 33rd row: K13, P3, K1
- 34th row: K4, P11, P2tog (16sts)
- 35th row: K12, P3, K1
- 36th row: K5, P9, P2tog (15sts)
- 37th row: K10, P4, K1
- 38th row: K5, P10
- 39th row: K2tog, K7, P5, K1 (14sts)
- 40th row: K6, P8
- 41st row: K8, P5, K1
- 42nd row: K7, P7

- 43rd row: K7, P6, K1
- 44th row: K7, P7
- 45th row: K7, P6, K1
- 46th row: Cast off 4, K2, P7 (10sts)
- 47th row: K7, put last 3 sts on pin for collar, turn –
- 48th row: P7
- Cast off

To make up: Join shoulder seams.
Catch top of centre back vent.

UPPER COLLAR

- Size 12/2.75mm

WORKING WITH WS FACING

- 1st row: K3 sts from left lapel, pick up 6 sts along left front neck, K9 from back neck, pick up 6 sts along right front neck, K3 sts from right lapel (27sts)
- 2nd row: K1, P25, K1
- 3rd row: K
- 4th row: Inc in 1st, P24, inc in next, K1 (29sts)
- 5th row: K9, inc in next, K9, inc in next, K8, inc in last (32sts)
- Cast off loosely

To make up: Steam press to tidy collar and lapels

JACKET SLEEVES –MAKE TWO

- Cast on 18
- Work 8 rows SS, starting with K
- 9th row: K row, inc in 1st and last st (20sts)
- Work 5 rows SS, starting with P
- 15th row: K row, inc in 1st and last st (22sts)
- Work 5 rows SS, starting with P

- 21st row: For left sleeve, K5, inc in next, K16 (23sts) For right sleeve, K15, inc in next, K6 (23sts)
- Work 8 rows SS, starting with P
- 30th row: Cast off 3, P to end (20sts)
- 31st row: Cast off 3, K to end (17sts)
- 32nd row: P
- 33rd row: K
- 34th row: P2tog, P13, P2tog (15sts)
- Work 3 rows SS, starting with K
- 38th row: P2tog, P11, P2tog (13sts)
- 39th row: K6, K2tog, K5 (12sts)
- 40th row: P2tog, P8, P2tog (10sts)
- 41st row: K
- 42nd row: Cast off, working first 2 sts together and last 2 sts together.

To make up: Join seams. Inset to jacket.
To finish the suit dress doll and add beads as front and cuff buttons.

CAP

COLOUR 7

- Size 12/2.75mm needle
- Size 12/2.75mm double-ended needle

CROWN

- Use 12/2.75mm double-ended

- Cast on 36
- Work 3 rows GS
- Join into circle
- 1st round: (inc in next, inc in next, K1)x12 (60sts)
- Work 6 rounds in K
- 8th round: (K2tog, K2tog, K1)x12 (36sts)
- Work 4 rounds in K
- 13th round: (K2togx4, K1)x4 (20sts)

- Work 4 rounds in K
- 18th round: K2tog to end (10sts)
- 19th round: K2tog to end (5sts)
- Pull wool through all stitches

BRIM

- Use 12/2.75mm needle

- Cast on 19
- 1st row: K19
- 2nd row: P18, turn –
- 3rd row: K17, turn –
- 4th row: P16, turn –
- 5th row: K15, turn –
- 6th row: P14, turn –
- 7th row: K13, turn –
- 8th row: P12, turn –
- 9th row: K11, turn –
- 10th row: P11, turn –
- 11th row: K12, turn –
- 12th row: P14, turn –
- 13th row: K16, turn –
- 14th row: P18
- Cast off

To make up: Stitch up garter stitch rows for cap band. Fold brim in half, joining cast on and cast off edges together and sew onto underside of crown. Stuff crown with wadding and steam to shape. Remove wadding.

TIE

COLOUR 8

- Size 12/2.75mm needles

- Cast on 6
- Work SS for 4 rows, starting with K
- 5th row: K1, K2tog, K2tog, K1 (4sts)

- 6th row: P
- Work 20 rows SS, starting with K
- 27th row: K1, K2tog, K1 (3sts)
- Continue in SS for 18 rows, starting with P
- Cast off

To make up: Steam press flat. Fold into a point at wide end and stitch in place. Fold in half and make a knot. Stitch in place. Add diagonal stripes of your choice in contrasting single strand wool using stem stitch.

HAIR AND WHISKERS

COLOUR 3 for hair use doubled
- Size 2.75mm needles
COLOUR 8 for whiskers

Tip: It is easier to fit hair and whiskers after the ears and nose have been placed and attached. See TO CREATE FACE.

HAIR
- Cast on 17
- 1st row: K
- 2nd row: P
- 3rd row: Inc in 1st, K15, inc in last (19sts)
- Continue in SS for 4 rows starting with P
- 8th row: Cast on 4, P 23 (23sts)
- 9th row: Cast on 4, K27 (27sts)
- Continue in SS for 3 rows
- Cast off

To make up: Fit to head. Stitch on. Create comb-over by stitching a few well placed lengths of wool across pate.

WHISKERS
Refer to a cartoon of your choice for expression. Fold a length of yarn over on itself 4 or 5 times to form a small skein 4-5cm in length. Secure at the centre and attach to face. Curve to shape (dampen fingers and tweak, allow to dry). Using sewing thread, stitch and shape loops together on both sides to form the moustache.

TO CREATE FACE
Refer to a cartoon of your choice to copy likeness. Add beads for eyes. The nose and ears are fashioned from crocheted chains of the flesh-coloured wool. Pin and stitch on when you feel you have a good likeness. Add eyebrows and mouth.

Maw's favourite room

You will need

MATERIALS:

Colour Codes:
1 Rowan Baby Merino Silk DK
(Shade 674 – Shell Pink) – For Body
2 Debbie Bliss Baby Cashmerino
(Shade 340068 – Flesh) – For Legs
3 Debbie Bliss Rialto 4ply
(Shade 22003 – Black) – For shoes
4 Rowan Fine Tweed
(Wensley Shade 371 – Teal) – For skirt
5 Debbie Bliss Rialto Lace
(Shade 44017 – Pale Blue) – For jumper
6 Debbie Bliss Rialto Lace
(Shade 44001 – Cream) – For collar and cuffs
7 Anchor Artiste Baby Soft
(Shade 07901 – White) – For Apron
8 John Lewis Own Baby 3-ply (White)
For Apron – (Used with 7 for apron strings)
9 Debbie Bliss Andes
(Shade 370019) – For Hair
10 Debbie Bliss Rialto Lace
(Shade 44003) – For Hair
11 Sirdar Snuggly DK brown – For Hair
(small amount needed)

Beads for eyes
Beads for brooch
Yarn for creating facial features
Reel of grey sewing thread
Stuffing
Small piece of beading wire

NEEDLES:

Size 10/3.25mm
Size 12/2.75mm
Size 12/2.75mm double-ended
Size 14/2mm
Size 14/2mm double-ended
Crochet hook 3.5mm
Darning needle

Maw

Weel, there's Maw, and she's a richt!
She works at hame frae morn tae nicht.
There's just ae family in her sicht –
The Broons!

Maw Broon is rarely seen without her pinny on, unless she is going out (to the pictures with her lassies or to the Women's Guild), when she wears a coat and sometimes a hat. A culinary queen when it comes to clootie dumpling, mince and tatties, and stovies. Has worn her hair in a bun since 1936. Her brusque exterior belies a love for jujube sweeties and a soppy film. A long-suffering and loving manager of the family.

BODY

COLOUR 1

- Size 10/3.25mm needles

BODY – FRONT

- Cast on 18
- 1st row: K
- 2nd row: P
- 3rd row: K1, inc in next, K14, inc in next, K1 (20sts)
- Work 5 rows SS, starting with P
- 9th row: K1, K2tog, K2, K2tog, K6, K2tog, K2, K2tog, K1 (16sts)
- Work 3 rows SS, starting with P
- 13th row: K2, inc in next, K10, inc in next, K2 (18sts)
- Work 3 rows SS, starting with P
- 17th row: K1, inc in next, K14, inc in next, K1 (20sts)
- Work 7 rows SS, starting with P
- 25th row: K1, sl1, K1, psso, K3, inc in next, K6, inc in next, K3, K2tog, K1 (20sts)
- Work 3 rows SS, starting with P
- 29th row: K1, sl1, K1, psso, K14, K2tog, K1 (18sts)
- 30th row: P
- 31st row: K1, sl1, K1, psso, K12, K2tog, K1 (16sts)
- 32nd row: P
- 33rd row: K1, sl1, K1, psso, K10, K2tog, K1 (14sts)
- 34th row: P
- 35th row: K1, sl1, K1, psso, K8, K2tog, K1 (12sts)
- Cast off

BODY – BACK

- Cast on 18

- 1st row: K
- 2nd row: P
- 3rd row: K2, inc in next, K1, inc in next, K8, inc in next, K1, inc in next, K2 (22sts)
- 4th row: P
- 5th row: K3, inc in next, K2, inc in next, K8, inc in next, K2, inc in next, K3 (26sts)
- Work 5 rows SS, starting with P
- 11th row: K2, K2tog, K18, K2tog, K2 (24sts)
- 12th row: P
- 13th row: (K2, K2tog)x2, K8, (K2tog, K2)x2 (20sts)
- 14th row: P
- 15th row: (K2, K2tog)x2, K4, (K2tog, K2)x2 (16sts)
- Work 9 rows SS, starting with P
- 25th row: K7, inc in next, inc in next, K7 (18sts)
- Work 7 rows SS, starting with P
- 33rd row: K1, sl1, K1, psso, K12, K2tog, K1 (16sts)
- 34th row: P
- 35th row: K1, sl1, K1, psso, K10, K2tog, K1 (14sts)
- 36th row: P
- 37th row: K1, sl1, K1, psso, K8, K2tog, K1 (12sts)
- Cast off

To make up: Join two pieces together. Stuff – do not overstuff.

UPPER TORSO/BUST – MAKE TWO

COLOUR 1

- Size 10/3.25mm needles
- Cast on 12
- 1st row: P

- 2nd row: K2tog, K8, K2tog (10sts)
- 3rd row: P
- 4th row: K2tog, K6, K2tog (8sts)
- 5th row: P2tog, P4, P2tog (6sts)
- 6th row: K2tog, K2, K2tog (4sts)
- Cast off
- The cast-on edge is the base of the triangles

CENTRAL BUST PANEL – MAKE ONE

COLOUR 1

- Size 10/3.25mm needles

- Cast on 15
- Work 3 rows SS, starting with K
- 4th row: P2tog, P11, P2tog (13sts)
- 5th row: K
- 6th row: P2tog, P9, P2tog (11sts)
- 7th row: K
- 8th row: P2tog, P7, P2tog (9sts)
- 9th row: K
- 10th row: P
- 11th row: K row – inc in 1st and last (11sts)
- 12th row: P
- 13th row: K row – inc in 1st and last (13sts)
- 14th row: P
- 15th row: K row – inc in 1st and last (15sts)
- Work 2 rows SS, starting with P
- Cast off

To make up: Stitch a triangle either end of the central bust panel to form a 'tent' shape. Attach to upper torso of body shape, leaving a small gap to push stuffing through. When happy with shape, sew-up the gap.

ARMS – MAKE TWO

COLOUR 1

- Size 10/3.25mm needles

WORKING FROM SHOULDER TO WRIST

- Cast on 5
- 1st row: K
- 2nd row: P
- 3rd row: K row – inc in 1st and last (7sts)
- 4th row: P
- 5th row: K row – inc in 1st and last (9sts)
- Work 29 rows SS, starting with P

TO CREATE LEFT HAND

- 35th row: K2, put 2 on pin, K5
- 36th row: P to end bringing 2 sections together (7sts)
- 37th row: K
- 38th row: P
- 39th row: K2tog, K2tog, K2tog, K1
- 40th row: P2tog, P2tog
- Pull thread through

TO CREATE RIGHT HAND

- 35th row: K5, put 2 on pin, K2 (7sts)
- 36th row: P
- 37th row: K
- 38th row: P
- 39th row: K1, K2tog, K2tog, K2tog
- 40th row: P2tog, P2tog
- Pull thread through

THUMB – SAME FOR BOTH HANDS

- Put 2sts from pin on size12/2.75mm double-ended needle
- Join thread, K2
- K2tog as i-cord
- Pull thread through

To make up: Join seams. Stuff. Attach to body.

LEGS – MAKE TWO

COLOUR 2

- Size 10/3.25mm needles

- Cast on 20
- 1st row: K7, K2tog, K2, K2tog, K7 (18sts)
- 2nd row: P8, P2tog, P8 (17sts)
- 3rd row: K
- 4th row:

Left leg: P2tog, P6, P2tog, P5, P2tog (14sts)

Right leg: P2tog, P5, P2tog, P6, P2tog (14sts)

- 5th row: K14
- 6th row: P4, cast off 6, P3 (8sts)
- 7th row: K across the 8sts, drawing them together
- Work 7 rows SS, starting with P
- 15th row: K1, inc in next, K4, inc in next, K1 (10sts)
- 16th row: P
- 17th row: K1, inc in next, K6, inc in next, K1 (12sts)
- 18th row: P
- 19th row: K1, inc in next, K8, inc in next, K1 (14sts)
- Work 7 rows SS, starting with P
- 27th row: K1, sl1, K1, psso, K8, K2tog, K1 (12sts)
- 28th row: P1, P2tog, P6, P2tog, P1 (10sts)
- Work 4 rows SS, starting with K
- 33rd row: K1, inc in next, K6, inc in next, K1 (12sts)
- Work 7 rows SS, starting with P
- 41st row: K1, inc in next, K8, inc in next, K1 (14sts)
- Work 7 rows SS, starting with P
- 49th row: K1, inc in next, K10, inc in next, K1 (16sts)
- Work 4 rows SS, starting with P
- Cast off

To make up: Join seams. Stuff. Attach to body.

HEAD

HEAD – FRONT
COLOUR 1

- Size 10/3.25mm needles

RIGHT SIDE OF FACE

- Cast on 5
- 1st row: K
- 2nd row: P
- 3rd row: Cast on 2, K to end (7sts)
- 4th row: P5, inc in next, inc in next (9sts)
- 5th row: K1, inc in next, inc in next, K6 (11sts)
- 6th row: P
- Break thread and leave on needle

LEFT SIDE OF FACE WITH WS FACING

- Cast on 5 – only work on these 5 sts
- 1st row: K
- 2nd row: P
- 3rd row: K to end, cast on 2 (7sts)
- 4th row: P1, inc in next, inc in next, P4 (9sts)
- 5th row: K6, inc in next, inc in next, K1 (11sts)
- 6th row: P11
- Now join 2 pieces together
- 7th row: K10, K2tog, K10 (21sts)
- 8th row: P1, P2tog, P15, P2tog, P1 (19sts)
- Work 6 rows SS, starting with K
- 15th row: K1, sl1, K1, psso, K13, K2tog, K1 (17sts)
- 16th row: P
- 17th row: K1, sl1, K1, psso, K11, K2tog, K1 (15sts)
- 18th row: P
- 19th row: K1, sl1, K1, psso, K9, K2tog, K1 (13sts)

- 20th row: P1, P2tog, P7, P2tog, P1 (11sts)
- 21st row: K1, sl1, K1, psso, K5, K2tog, K1 (9sts)
- 22nd row: P
- Cast off

HEAD – BACK

- Cast on 6
- 1st row: K
- 2nd row: P
- 3rd row: K row – inc in 1st and last (8sts)
- 4th row: P
- 5th row: K row – inc in 1st and last (10sts)
- 6th row: P
- 7th row: K row – inc in 1st and last (12sts)
- 8th row: P
- 9th row: K row – inc in 1st and last (14sts)
- Work 8 rows SS, starting with P
- 18th row: P2tog, P10, P2tog (12sts)
- 19th row: K
- 20th row: P2tog, P8, P2tog (10sts)
- 21st row: K
- Cast off

SKIRT

COLOUR 4

- Size 11/3.00mm needles

- Cast on 46
- Work 10 rows SS, starting with K
- 11th row: Cast off 3, K42 (43sts)
- Work 7 rows SS, starting with P
- 19th row: K11, inc in next, K19, inc in next, K11 (45sts)
- Work 9 rows SS, starting with P
- 29th row: K12, inc in next, K19, inc in next, K12 (47sts)
- Work 3 rows starting with P

- 33rd row: K6, inc in next, K33, inc in next, K6 (49sts)
- Work 3 rows SS, starting with P
- 37th row: K7, inc in next, K33, inc in next, K7 (51sts)
- Work 3 rows SS, starting with P
- 41st row: K14, K2tog, K19, K2tog, K14 (49sts)
- Work 3 rows SS, starting with P
- 45th row: K6, K2tog, K5, K2tog, K19, K2tog, K5, K2tog, K6 (45sts)
- 46th row: P
- 47th row: K4, K2tog, K4, K2tog, K1, K2tog, K15, K2tog, K1, K2tog, K4, K2tog, K4 (39sts)
- 48th row: P
- 49th row: K10, K2tog, K15, K2tog, K10 (37sts)
- Cast off

To make up: Press under damp cloth. Join centre seam at back, leaving kick-pleat open.

JUMPER

COLOUR 5

- Size 12/2.75mm needles

JUMPER BACK

- Cast on 28
- Work 4 rows 1 and 1 rib
- Work 23 rows SS, starting with K
- 28th row: Cast off 1, P to end (27sts)
- 29th row: Cast off 1, K to end (26sts)
- 30th row: P
- 31st row: K2tog, K22, K2tog (24sts)
- Work 5 rows SS, starting with P
- 37th row: K7 turn –
- 38th row: P7
- 39th row: K6, K2tog, K16 (23sts)
- 40th row: P7

- 41st row: K7
- Cast off working 7th and 8th sts together

JUMPER FRONT

- Cast on 28
- Work 4 rows 1 and 1 rib
- Work 4 rows SS, starting with K
- 9th row: K1, inc in next, K24, inc in next, K1 (30sts)
- Work 5 rows SS, starting with P
- 15th row: K1, inc in next, K26, inc in next, K1 (32sts)
- Work 3 rows SS, starting with P
- 19th row: K1, inc in next, K28, inc in next, K1 (34sts)
- Work 3 rows SS, starting with P
- 23rd row: K2tog, K30, K2tog (32sts)

- Word 4 rows SS, starting with P
- 28th row: Cast off 2, P to end (30sts)
- 29th row: Cast off 2, K to end (28sts)
- 30th row: P
- 31st row: K2tog, K24, K2tog (26sts)
- Work 2 rows SS, starting with P
- 34th row: P2tog, P22, P2tog (24sts)
- Work 5 rows SS, starting with K
- 40th row: P2tog, P7, turn –
- 41st row: K2tog, K6
- 42nd row: P7, turn –
- 43rd row: K7
- 44th row: Cast off 3, P3, turn –
- Cast off 4
- Put next 6 sts on pin
- With WS facing, join wool at neck edge to work on left side front
- 40th row: P7, P2tog (8sts)
- 41st row: K6, K2tog (7sts)
- Work 3 rows SS, starting with P
- 45th row: Cast off 3, K3
- Cast off

COLLAR

COLOUR 6
- Size 12/2.75mm double-ended needles

JOIN SHOULDER SEAMS AND WITH RS FACING, STARTING AT CENTRE FRONT
- 1st row: K3 sts from pin at right front neck, pick up 8 sts along right front neck, pick up 14 along the back neck, pick up 8 along left front neck and K remaining 3 sts from pin, turn – (36sts)
- 2nd row: K1, P34, K1, turn –
- 3rd row: K, turn –
- 4th row: K1, P34, K1, turn –
- 5th row: K1, inc in next, K9, inc in next, K12,

inc in next, K9, inc in next, K1, turn – (38sts)
- 6th row: K1, P36, K1 turn –
- 7th row: K, turn –
- Cast off

SLEEVES – MAKE TWO

COLOURS 6 and 5
- Size 12/2.75mm needles

- Cast on 24 using COLOUR 6
- Work 5 rows SS, starting with K
- Join in COLOUR 5 and work 9 rows SS, starting with P
- 15th row: K1, inc in next, K20, inc in next, K1 (26sts)
- Work 7 rows SS, starting with P
- 23rd row: K1, inc in next, K22, inc in next, K1 (28sts)
- Work 6 rows SS, starting with P
- 30th row: Cast off 2, P to end (26sts)
- 31st row: Cast off 2, K to end (24sts)
- 32nd row: P
- 33rd row: K2tog, K18, turn –
- 34th row: P16, turn –
- 35th row: K15, K2tog, K1, K2tog
- 36th row: P17, P2tog, P2 (20sts)
- 37th row: K16, turn –
- 38th row: P12, turn –
- 39th row: K11, K2tog, K3
- Cast off

To make up: Press under damp cloth. Join seams. Inset in jumper. Dress doll.

APRON

COLOURS 7 and 8
- Size 12/2.75mm needles

WORKING FROM HEM TO WAISTBAND
- Cast on 24 in COLOUR 7
- Work 33 rows SS, starting with K, all P rows have K1 at each end
- 34th row: P
- 35th row: P
- 36th row: K
- 37th row: K
- Cast off

To make up: Work chain stitch length to make ties at each end of waistband working COLOURS 7 and 8 together. Tie round waist of doll and form a bow.

SHOES – MAKE TWO

COLOUR 3
- Size 12/2.75mm needles

- Cast on 17
- 1st row: K10, turn –
- 2nd row: P7, turn –
- 3rd row: K14
- 4th row: P17
- 5th row: K10, turn –
- 6th row: P7, turn –
- 7th row: K14
- 8th row: P14, turn –
- 9th row: K14
- 10th row: Cast off 12, P4 (5sts)
- 11th row: K2tog, K3 (4sts)
- 12th row: P
- 13th row: Inc in 1st, K3, cast on 12 (17sts)
- 14th row: P14, turn –
- 15th row: K7, turn –
- 16th row: P10
- 17th row: K17
- 18th row: P14, turn –

- 19th row: K7, turn –
- 20th row: P10
- 21st row: K17
- Cast off

HEEL
- Sew up centre back heel seam
- Cast on 3, with RS facing pick up 6 sts across back heel, cast on 3 (12sts)
- 1st row: P
- 2nd row: (K3, K2tog)x3, K3 (9sts)
- 3rd row: (P2tog)x2, P1, (P2tog)x2 (5sts)
- Cast off

To make up: Press flat under damp cloth. Fold and working inside out close heel seam of shoe and continue stitching along base. At toe, turn shoe right-side out and make 1 or 2 finishing stitches at pointed toe.
Place on foot – a catching stitch will ensure it stays on. If the upper edge of shoe sits too loose, run a length of single strand yarn all round the upper edge. Pull gently and fasten off to fit.

NOSE
COLOUR 1
- Size 10/3.25 needles

- Cast on 5
- 1st row: K
- 2nd row: P
- 3rd row: K2tog, K1, K2tog (3sts)
- 4th row: P
- 5th row: K
- Cut yarn, draw through last 3 sts and fasten off.

To make up: Fold and stitch in place.

HAIR
COLOUR 9

Tip: It is easier to work on hair after the ears have been placed. See TO CREATE FACE.

TO COVER CROWN SECTION
Cut a generous length of wool. Secure at nape of neck and run yarn from nape to front of hairline, backwards and forwards, catching in place with sewing thread. Cut more yarn and repeat until central portion of crown is covered.

SIDES OF HEAD
Cut lengths of yarn approx 34cm in length. Fold each length over a few times to form small, uncut hanks measuring approx. 8.5cm. These hanks will form the sides and bun. Attach uncut ends to the hairline to frame the face using sewing thread. Gather hanks in at the back, twist to form bun and secure with a few stitches.
Using the crochet hook, hook in and tie added pieces of COLOUR 10 and strands of COLOUR 11 so that Maw Broon has a 'salt and pepper' look. Pay particular attention around the hairline where the hair frames the face.

TO CREATE FACE
The ears are crocheted chains of flesh colour, wound round and stitched to shape. Add beads for eyes and use your own choice of yarn for brows and mouth. Maw Broon is the lynch pin of the family. Refer to a cartoon of your choice for a typical expression.

BROOCH
Thread chosen brooch beads onto fine wire. Form a circle, twist wire and trim ends. Twist in a larger bead in a contrasting colour in the centre. Add to centre front of jumper at throat.

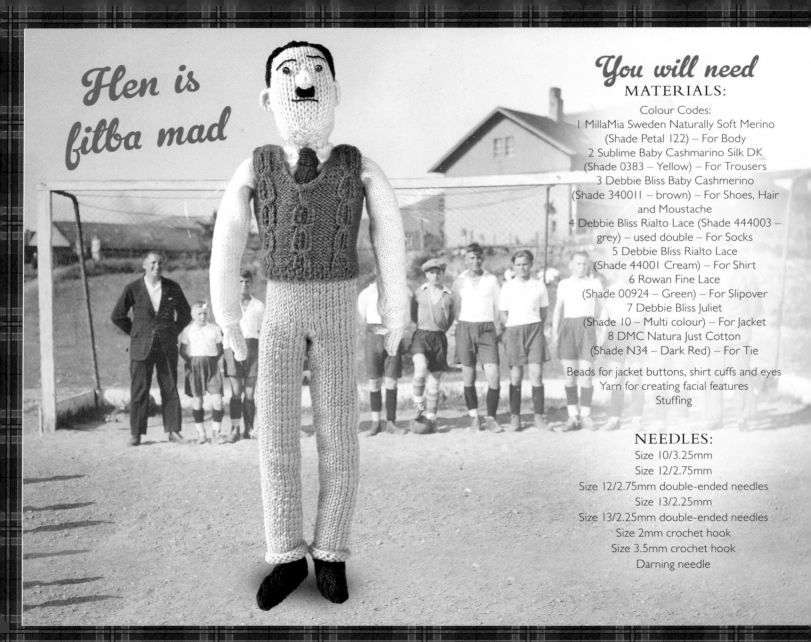

Hen is filba mad

You will need
MATERIALS:
Colour Codes:
1 MillaMia Sweden Naturally Soft Merino
(Shade Petal 122) – For Body
2 Sublime Baby Cashmarino Silk DK
(Shade 0383 – Yellow) – For Trousers
3 Debbie Bliss Baby Cashmerino
(Shade 340011 – brown) – For Shoes, Hair
and Moustache
4 Debbie Bliss Rialto Lace (Shade 444003 –
grey) – used double – For Socks
5 Debbie Bliss Rialto Lace
(Shade 44001 Cream) – For Shirt
6 Rowan Fine Lace
(Shade 00924 – Green) – For Slipover
7 Debbie Bliss Juliet
(Shade 10 – Multi colour) – For Jacket
8 DMC Natura Just Cotton
(Shade N34 – Dark Red) – For Tie

Beads for jacket buttons, shirt cuffs and eyes
Yarn for creating facial features
Stuffing

NEEDLES:
Size 10/3.25mm
Size 12/2.75mm
Size 12/2.75mm double-ended needles
Size 13/2.25mm
Size 13/2.25mm double-ended needles
Size 2mm crochet hook
Size 3.5mm crochet hook
Darning needle

Hen

Unusually tall and skinny for a Scotsman, Hen Broon has been the subject of much graffiti in his time. Usually wears a striped suit and a bowler hat, unless he's having his tea. Joined the army during World War II. Has had varied success with the ladies, who often have to stand on the close stairs to be able to reach him to give him a wee kiss. He has a bottomless stomach for one so lanky.

Hen is tired of being thin,
a bag of skin and bone,
He wishes for big muscles,
like footballs fully blown.
To be like Mr Universe,
is Hen Broon's greatest goal.
Then not a sowel could call him,
the walkin' greenie-pole.

BODY

COLOUR 1
- Size 10/3.25mm needles

BODY – FRONT
- Cast on 14
- 1st row: K
- 2nd row: P
- 3rd row: K1 inc in next, K10, inc in next, K1 (16sts)
- Work 7 rows SS, starting with P
- 11th row: K1, K2tog, K2, K2tog, K2, K2tog, K2, K2tog, K1 (12sts)
- Work 7 rows SS, starting with P
- 19th row: K2, inc in next, K6, inc in next, K2 (14sts)
- 20th row: P
- 21st row: Inc in 1st, K3, inc in next, K4, inc in next, K3, inc in last (18sts)
- 22nd row: P
- 23rd row: K5, inc in next, K6, inc in next, K5 (20sts)
- 24th row: P
- 25th row: K6, inc in next, K6, inc in next, K6 (22sts)
- 26th row: P
- 27th row: K1, K2tog, K16, K2tog, K1 (20sts)
- Work 9 rows SS, starting with P
- 37th row: K1, sl1, K1, psso, K14, K2tog, K1 (18sts)
- 38th row: P1, P2tog, P12, P2tog, P1 (16sts)
- 39th row: K
- 40th row: P
- Cast off

BODY – BACK
- Cast on 14
- 1st row: K

- 2nd row: P
- 3rd row: K
- 4th row: P
- 5th row: K2, inc in next, K1, inc in next, K4, inc in next, K1, inc in next, K2 (18sts)
- Work 3 rows SS, starting with P
- 9th row: K3, inc in next, K1, inc in next, K6, inc in next, K1, inc in next, K3 (22sts)
- Work 5 rows SS, starting with P
- 15th row: K1, K2tog, K16, K2tog, K1 (20sts)
- 16th row: P
- 17th row: K2, K2tog, K1, K2tog, K6, K2tog, K1, K2tog, K2 (16sts)
- 18th row: P
- 19th row: K2, K2tog, K2, K2tog, K2tog, K2, K2tog, K2 (12sts)
- Work 5 rows SS, starting with P
- 25th row: K1, inc in next, K3, inc in next, inc in next, K3, inc in next, K1 (16sts)
- Work 11 rows SS, starting with P
- 37th row: K1, inc in next, K12, inc in next, K1 (18sts)
- 38th row: P
- 39th row: K1, sl1, K1, psso, K12, K2tog, K1 (16sts)
- 40th row: P1, P2tog, P10, P2tog, P1 (14sts)
- 41st row: K
- 42nd row: P
- Cast off

To make up: Join front and back. Stuff.

HEAD

COLOUR 1
- Size 10/3.25mm needles

RIGHT SIDE OF FACE
- Cast on 5

- 1st row: P
- 2nd row: K
- 3rd row: P
- 4th row: Cast on 2, K to end (7sts)
- 5th row: P5, inc in next, inc in next (9sts)
- 6th row: Inc in 1st, inc in next, K7 (11sts)
- 7th row: P11
- Break thread and leave on spare needle

LEFT SIDE OF FACE
- Cast on 5
- 1st row: P
- 2nd row: K
- 3rd row: P
- 4th row: K to end, cast on 2 (7sts)
- 5th row: Inc in 1st, inc in next, P5 (9sts)
- 6th row: K7, inc in next, inc in next (11sts)
- 7th row: P11
- Now join 2 pieces together
- 8th row: K10, K last of left side and 1st of right side tog, K10 (21sts)
- 9th row: P1, P2tog, P15, P2tog, P1 (19sts)
- Work 8 rows SS, starting with K
- 18th row: K2tog, K15, K2tog (17sts)
- 19th row: P
- 20th row: K2tog, K13, K2tog (15sts)
- 21st row: P
- 22nd row: K2tog, K11, K2tog (13sts)
- 23rd row: P2tog, P9, P2tog (11sts)
- 24th row: K2tog, K7, K2tog (9sts)
- Cast off

HEAD – BACK
- Cast on 6
- 1st row: P
- 2nd row: K
- 3rd row: P
- 4th row: K row – inc in 1st and last (8sts)

- 5h row: P
- 6th row: K row – inc in 1st and last (10sts)
- 7th row: P
- 8th row: K row – inc in 1st and last (12sts)
- 9th row: P
- 10th row: K row – inc in 1st and last (14sts)
- Work 9 rows SS, starting with P
- 20th row: K2tog, K10, K2tog (12sts)
- 21st row: P
- 22nd row: K2tog, K8, K2tog (10sts)
- Cast off

To make up: Join front to back. Stuff.

ARMS – MAKE TWO

COLOUR 1
- Size 10/3.25mm needles
- Size 12/2.75mm double-ended needles

WORKING FROM SHOULDER TO WRIST
- Cast on 5
- 1st row: K
- 2nd row: P
- 3rd row K row – inc in 1st and last (7sts)
- 4th row: P
- 5th row: K row – inc in 1st and last (9sts)
- Work 37 rows SS, starting with P

FOR LEFT HAND
- 43rd row: K2, put 2sts on pin, K5 (7sts)
- Work 4 rows SS, starting with P
- 48th row: P2tog, P2tog, P2tog, P1 (4sts)
- 49th row: K2tog, K2tog (2sts)
- Pull wool through

FOR RIGHT HAND
- 43rd row: K5, put 2sts on pin, K2 (7sts)
- Work 4 rows SS, starting with P

- 48th row: P1, P2tog, P2tog, P2tog (4sts)
- 49th row: K2tog, K2tog (2sts)
- Pull wool through

THUMB – SAME FOR BOTH HANDS
- Join wool to 2sts on pin
- Use size 12/2.75mm double-ended needles to work i-cord for 3 rows
- Pull wool through and darn end

To make up: Join seams. Stuff. Attach to body

LEGS – MAKE TWO

COLOUR 3
- Size 10/3.25mm needles

- Cast on 28
- 1st row: K
- 2nd row: P
- 3rd row: K12, K2tog, K2tog, K12 (26sts)
- 4th row: P12, P2tog, P12 (25sts)
- 5th row: K7, (K2tog, K1)x3, K2tog, K7 (21sts)
- 6th row: P
- 7th row: K5, cast off 10, K5 (11sts)
- 8th row: P5, P2tog, P4 (10sts)
- Join in COLOUR 4
- Work 6 rows SS, starting with K
- 15th row: K1, inc in next, K6, inc in next, K1 (12sts)
- 16th row: P
- Join in COLOUR 1
- Work 51 rows SS, starting with K
- Cast off

To make up: Sew-up sole of boot. Stuff boot with offcuts of brown wool rather than white wadding, which tends to show through. Sew leg seams. Attach to body

SHIRT

COLOUR 5

- Size 13/2.25mm needles
- Size 13/2.25mm double-ended needles

MAIN BODY OF SHIRT

- Cast on 66
- 1st row: K
- 2nd row: K2, P62, K2
- Repeat rows 1 and 2 (x12)
- 27th row: K17, cast off 2, K27, cast off 2, K16 (62sts)

FRONT LEFT SIDE – WITH WS FACING

WORKING ON 17STS – PUT REMAINING STS ON PIN

- Work 14 rows SS, starting with P – Each P row starting with K2
- 15th row: Cast off 3, P to end (14sts)
- 16th row: K14
- 17th row: Cast off 2, P to end (12sts)
- 18th row: Cast off 5, K to end (7sts)
- 19th row: P
- Cast off 7
- Pull wool through

BACK – WITH WS FACING

- Working on next 28sts from pin:
- Work 16 rows SS, starting with P
- 17th row: Cast off 11, P16 (17sts)
- 18th row: Cast off 11 and leave remaining 6sts on pin for collar

FRONT RIGHT SIDE – WITH WS FACING

- Working on remaining 17sts
- Work 13 rows SS, starting with P – Each P row ending with K2

- 14th row: Cast off 3, K to end (14sts)
- 15th row: P all sts
- 16th row: Cast off 2, K to end (12sts)
- 17th row: Cast off 5, P to end (7sts)
- 18th row: K
- Cast off

Join shoulder seams

COLLAR – WITH RS FACING

- Pick up 11 sts along right front neck, K6 from pin across back neck, pick up 11 sts along left front neck (28sts), turn –
- With WS facing
- 1st row: K
- 2nd row: K1, P26, K1
- 3rd row: K
- 4th row: K1, P26, K1
- 5th row: K1, inc in next, K5, inc in next, K1, inc in next, K8, inc in next, K1, inc in next, K5, inc in next, K1 (34sts)
- 6th row: K1, P32, K1
- 7th row: K
- 8th row: K1, P32, K1
- 9th row: K33, inc in last (35sts)
- Cast off

SLEEVES

LEFT SLEEVE – WORKING FROM SHOULDER TO WRIST

- Cast on 30
- Work 11 rows SS, starting with K
- 12th row: P1, P2tog, P24, P2tog, P1 (28sts)
- Work 11 rows SS, starting with K
- 24th row: P1, P2tog, P22, P2tog, P1 (26sts)
- Work 11 rows SS, starting with K
- 36th row: P1, P2tog, P20, P2tog, P1 (24sts)
- Work 20 rows SS, starting with K

- 57th row: K this row onto 3 double-ended needles
- 58th row: P6, turn –
- 59th row: K6, K18 from other end of needles (this closes the underarm seam and gives a vent opening at the side back), turn –
- 60th row: P
- 61st row: K
- 62nd row: P
- 63rd row: K3, (K2tog, K2) x2, K2tog, K1, (K2tog)x4, K2 (17sts)
- 64th row: K17, cast on 3 (20sts) – this makes the cuff in reverse SS
- 65th row: K1, P18, K1
- 66th row: K
- 67th row: K1, P18, K1
- 68th row: K
- 69th row: K1, P18, K1
- 70th row: K
- Cast off

RIGHT SLEEVE – WORKING FROM SHOULDER TO WRIST

- Cast on 30
- Work 11 rows SS, starting with K
- 12th row: P1, P2tog, P24, P2tog, P1 (28sts)
- Work 11 rows SS, starting with K
- 24th row: P1, P2tog, P22, P2tog, P1 (26sts)
- Work 11 rows SS, starting with K
- 36th row: P1, P2tog, P20, P2tog, P1 (24sts)
- Work 20 rows SS, starting with K
- 57th row: K this row onto 3 double-ended needles
- 58th row: P18, turn –
- 59th row: K18, K6 from other end of needles (this closes the underarm seam and gives a vent opening at the side back), turn –
- 60th row: P

- 61st row: K
- 62nd row: P
- 63rd row: K2, (K2tog) x4, K1, K2tog, (K2, K2tog) x2, K3 (17sts)
- 64th row: Cast on 3, knit to end (20sts) – this makes the cuff in reverse SS
- 65th row: K1, P18, K1
- 66th row: K
- 67th row: K1, P18, K1
- 68th row: K
- 69th row: K1, P18, K1
- 70th row: K
- Cast off

To make up: Sew up sleeve seams and inset sleeves. Dress doll and lace front together with COLOUR 5. Add beads as shirt cuff buttons.

TROUSERS

COLOUR 2
- Size 10/3.25mm needles

RIGHT LEG
- Cast on 19
- Work 24 rows SS, starting with K
- 25th row: K row, inc in next, K9 (20sts)
- Work 15 rows SS, starting with P
- 41st row: K9, inc in next, K10 (21sts)
- Work 15 rows SS, starting with P
- 57th row: K10, inc in next, K10 (22sts)
- Work 5 rows SS, starting with P
- 63rd row: Inc in 1st, K10, inc in next, K9, inc in last (25sts)
- Work 5 rows SS, starting P
- 69th row: K12, inc in next, K12 (26sts)
- 70th row: Cast off 2, P to end (24sts)
- 71st row: Cast off 2, K to end (22sts)
- 72nd row: P, hold on pin

LEFT LEG
- Cast on 19
- Work as right leg to row 72

- Knitting legs together, starting with left leg:
- 73rd row: K2tog, K3, inc in next, K15, K last stitch of left leg with first stitch of right leg, K15, inc in next, K3, K2tog (43sts)
- Work 10 rows SS, starting with P
- 84th row: P6, P2tog, P4, P2tog, P15, P2tog, P4, P2tog, P6 (39sts)
- 85th row: K
- Join in COLOUR 3
- 86th row: P
- 87th row: P
- Join in COLOUR 2
- 88th row: P
- 89th row: K
- Cast off

To make up: Join leg and crotch seams. Add to doll.

SLIPOVER

COLOUR 6 USE DOUBLED
- Size 12/2.75mm needles

FRONT
- Cast on 36
- Work 4 rows 1 and 1 rib
- 5th row: P7, K1, P2, K1, P5, K1, P2, K1, P5, K1, P2, K1, P7
- 6th row: K7, P1, K2, P1, K5, P1, K2, P1, K5, P1, K2, P1, K7
- 7th row: As row 5
- 8th row: K7, (put next st onto cable pin to back, K1, P from cable pin, put next st on cable pin to front, P1, K from cable pin, K5) x3, K2
- 9th row: P8, K2, (P7, K2) x2, P8
- 10th row: K7, (put next st onto cable pin to front, P1, K from cable pin, put next st on cable pin to back, K1, P from cable pin, K5) x3, K2
- 11th row: As row 5
- 12th row: As row 6
- 13th row: As row 5
- 14th row: As row 6
- 15th row: As row 5
- 16th row: As row 8
- 17th row: As row 9
- 18th row: As row 10
- 19th row: As row 5
- 20th row: As row 6
- 21st row: As row 5
- 22nd row: As row 6
- 23rd row: As row 5
- 24th row: As row 8
- 25th row: As row 9
- 26th row: K7, *put next st onto cable pin to front, P1, K from cable pin, put next st on cable pin to back, K1, P from cable pin*, K6, P2, K6, repeat from * to *, K7
- 27th row: P7, K1, P2, K1, P6, K2, P6, K1, P2, K1, P7
- 28th row: Cast off 4, K2, P1, K2, P1, K6, cast off 2, K5, P1, K2, P1, K7
- 29th row: Cast off 4, P2, k1, P2, K1, P6, turn – (13sts)
- NOW WORKING ON THE LEFT FRONT
- 30th row: K2tog, K4, P1, K2, P1, K1, K2tog (11sts)
- 31st row: P2, K1, P2, K1, P5
- 32nd row: K5, put next st onto cable pin to back, K1, P from cable pin, put next st on cable pin to front, P1, K from cable pin, K2

- 33rd row: P3, K2, P4, P2tog (10sts)
- 34th row: K4, put next st onto cable pin to front, P1, K from cable pin, put next st on cable pin to back, K1, P from cable pin, K2
- 35th row: P2, K1, P2, K1, P4
- 36th row: K4, P1, K2, P1, K2
- 37th row: P2, K1, P2, K1, P2, P2tog (9sts)
- 38th row: K3, P1, K2, P1, K2
- 39th row: P2, K1, P2, K1, P3
- 40th row: K3, P1, K2, P1, K2
- 41st row: P2, sl1, K1, psso, K2tog, P3 (7sts)
- 42nd row: K3, P2, K2
- 43rd row: P2, K2, P3
- Cast off
- Rejoin wool with RS facing to centre front – NOW WORKING ON RIGHT SIDE
- 29th row: P6, K1, P2, K1, P3 (13sts)
- 30th row: K2tog, K1, P1, K2, P1, K4, K2tog (11sts)
- 31st row: P5, K1, P2, K1, P2
- 32nd row: K2, put next st onto cable pin to back, K1, P from cable pin, put next st on cable pin to front, P1, K from cable pin, K5
- 33rd row: P2tog, P4, K2, P3 (10sts)
- 34th row: K2, put next st onto cable pin to front, P1, K from cable pin, put next st on cable pin to back, K1, P from cable pin, K4
- 35th row: P4, K1, P2, K1, P2
- 36th row: K2, P1, K2, P1, K4
- 37th row: P2tog, P2, K1, P2, K1, P2 (9sts)
- 38th row: K2, P1, K2, P1, K3
- 39th row: P3, K1, P2, K1, P2
- 40th row: K2, P1, K2, P1, K3
- 41st row: P3, sl1, K1, psso, K2tog, P2 (7sts)
- 42nd row: K2, P2, K3
- 43rd row: P3, K2, P2
- Cast off

BACK
COLOUR 6
- Size 12/2.75mm needles

- Cast on 30
- Work 4 rows 1 and 1 rib
- Work 7 rows SS, starting with P – this is worked in reverse SS
- 12th row: K2tog, K26, K2tog (28sts)
- 13th row: P
- 14th row: K2tog, K24, K2tog (26sts)
- 15th row: P
- 16th row: K
- 17th row: P row inc in 1st and last (28sts)
- 18th row: K
- 19th row: P row inc in 1st and last (30sts)
- Work 7 rows SS, starting with K
- 27th row: Cast off 2, P to end (28sts)
- 28th row: Cast off 2, K to end (26sts)
- 29th row: P2tog, P22, P2tog (24sts)
- 30th row: K
- 31st row: P2tog, P20, p2tog (22sts)
- Work 9 rows SS, starting K
- 41st row: P8, turn –
- 42nd row: K8
- 43rd row: Cast off 4, P to end
- 44th row: K8, turn –
- 45th row: P8
- Cast off

To make up: Join front to back at side seams and shoulder seams. Dress doll. Use 2mm crochet hook and a length of yarn to finish off and tidy the armholes and neck edge with reverse single chain edging.

JACKET
COLOUR 7
- Size 10/3.25mm needles

FRONT AND BACK – LEFT
- Cast on 26
- 1st row: K
- 2nd row: K1, P24, K1
- 3rd row: K
- 4th row: K1, P24, K1
- 5th row: K
- 6th row: K1, P24, K1
- 7th row: K
- 8th row: K1, P24, K1
- 9th row: K
- 10th row: K1, P24, K1
- 11th row: K
- 12th row: K1, P24, K1
- Set aside on pin

FRONT AND BACK – RIGHT
- Cast on 28
- 1st row: K
- 2nd row: K1, P26, K1
- 3rd row: K
- 4th row: K1, P26, K1
- 5th row: K
- 6th row: K1, P26, K1
- 7th row: K
- 8th row: K1, P26, K1
- 9th row: K
- 10th row: K1, P26, K1
- 11th row: K
- 12th row: Cast off 2, P24, K1 (26sts)

TO JOIN JACKET PIECES TOGETHER
- With RS facing work row 13 across front and back right, followed by front and back left
- 13th row: K25, K last stitch from right side and first from left side together, K25 (51sts)

- 14th row: K1, P11, P2tog, P23, P2tog, P11, K1 (49sts)
- 15th row: K
- 16th row: K1, P47, K1
- 17th row: K
- 18th row: K1, P13, P2tog, P17, P2tog, P13, K1 (47sts)
- 19th row: K
- 20th row: K1, P45, K1
- 21st row: K
- 22nd row: K1, P45, K1
- 23rd row: K14, inc in next, K17, inc in next, K14 (49sts)
- 24th row: K1, P47, K1
- 25th row: K12, inc in next, K23, inc in next, K12 (51sts)
- 26th row: K1, P49, K1
- 27th row: K1, inc in next, K47, inc in next, K1 (53sts)
- 28th row: K2, P49, K2
- 29th row: K1, P1, K49, P1, K1
- 30th row: K3, P47, K3
- 31st row: K1, P2, K47, P2, K1
- 32nd row: K3, P47, K3
- 33rd row: K1, P2, K47, P2, K1
- 34th row: K4, P45, K4
- 35th row: K1, P3, K10, cast off 2, K20, cast off 2, K9, P3, K1 (49sts)

NOW WORKING ON LEFT FRONT, 14 STS
- 36th row: K4, P8, P2tog (13sts)
- 37th row: K9, P3, K1
- 38th row: K5, P8
- 39th row: K8, P4, K1
- 40th row: K5, P6, P2tog (12sts)
- 41st row: K7, P4, K1
- 42nd row: K6, P6
- 43rd row: K6, P5, K1

- 44th row: Cast off 4, K1, P6 (8sts)
- 45th row: K6, put last 2 sts on pin for collar, turn –
- 46th row: P6
- Cast off

WORKING ON JACKET BACK – NEXT 21 STS – WS FACING
- 36th row: P
- 37th row: K
- 38th row: P2tog, P17, P2tog (19sts)
- Work 7 rows SS, starting K
- 46th row: Cast off 6, P12 (13sts)
- 47th row: Cast off 6, put remaining sts on pin for collar

WORKING ON FRONT RIGHT – REMAINING 14 STS – WS FACING
- 36th row: P2tog, P8, K4 (13sts)
- 37th row: K1, P3, K9
- 38th row: P8, K5
- 39th row: K1, P4, K8
- 40th row: P2tog, P6, K5 (12sts)
- 41st row: K1, P4, K7
- 42nd row: P6, K6
- 43rd row: K1, P5, K6
- 44th row: P6, K6
- 45th row: Cast off 4, P1, K6 (8sts)
- 46th row: P6, put last 2 sts on pin for collar, turn –
- 47th row: K6
- 48th row: P6
- Cast off

To make up: Join shoulder seams. Catch top of centre back vent.

UPPER COLLAR
- Size 12/2.75mm needles

WORKING WITH WS FACING
- 1st row: K2 sts from left lapel, pick up 6 sts along left front neck, K7 from back neck, pick up 6 sts along right front neck, K2 sts from right lapel (23sts)
- 2nd row: K1, P21, K1
- 3rd row: K
- 4th row: K1, inc in next, P19, inc in next, K1 (25sts)
- 5th row: K9, inc in next, K5, inc in next, K8, inc in last (28sts)
- Cast off loosely

To make up: Steam press to tidy collar and lapels.

JACKET SLEEVES – MAKE TWO

- Cast on 14
- Work 14 rows SS, starting with K
- 15th row: K row, inc in 1st and last st (16sts)
- Work 7 rows SS, starting with P
- 23rd row: For left sleeve, K3, inc in next, K12 (17sts) For right sleeve, K11, inc in next, K4 (17sts)
- Work 10 rows SS, starting with P
- 34th row: Cast off 2, P to end (15sts)
- 35th row: Cast off 2, K to end (13sts)
- 36th row: P2tog, P9, P2tog (11sts)
- Work 4 rows SS, starting with K
- 41st row: K2tog, K7, K2tog (9sts)
- 42nd row: P2tog, P5, P2tog (7sts)
- 43rd row: K
- Cast off

To make up: Join seams. Inset to jacket. Dress doll and add beads as front and cuff buttons.

TIE

COLOUR 8

- Size 12/2.75mm needles

- Cast on 3
- Work 28 rows SS, starting with K
- 29th row: K1, inc in next, K1 (4sts)
- Work 14 rows SS, starting with P
- 44th row: K1, inc in next, inc in next, K1 (6sts)
- Work 24 rows SS, starting with P
- 69th row: K2tog, K2, K2tog (4sts)
- 70th row: P
- 71st row: K2tog, K2tog (2sts)
- Cut yarn and pull wool through

To make up: Steam press under a damp cloth. Decide where knot should sit. Wind round twice to form knot and stitch in place.

HAIR

COLOUR 3

- Size 10/3.25mm needles

Tip: Make and attach ears and nose before adding hair – see TO CREATE FACE.

- Cast on 12
- Work 4 rows SS, starting with K
- 5th row: K1, inc in next, K8, inc in next, K1 (14sts)
- Work 3 rows SS, starting with P
- 9th row: Cast on 3, K17 (17sts)
- 10th row: Cast on 3, P20 (20sts)
- 11th row: K6, K2tog, K4, K2tog, K6 (18sts)
- 12th row: P
- 13th row: Cast off 4, K13 (14sts)
- 14th row: Cast off 4, P9 (10sts)
- 15th row: K2tog, K6, K2tog (8sts)
- 16th row: P2tog, P4, P2tog (6sts)
- 17th row: K2tog, K2tog, K2tog (3sts)
- 18th row: P
- 19th row: K
- Cut thread and draw through last 3 sts. Pull tight and fasten off.

To make up: Attach to head to form short back and sides. Use a darning needle and lengths of yarn to create a combed back look by working stitches of differing lengths running from hairline to back of crown.

TO CREATE FACE

NOSE AND EARS

Using 3.5mm crochet hook, make a chain of 7sts. Join in a circle then make a further chain of 4sts. The ears are formed from a crocheted chain curled around on itself and stitched. Attach to face.

Add beads for eyes. Add mouth and brows in yarn of choice. Our Hen wears a very quizzical look

Joe's the life and soul o' a ceilidh!

BUTTON ACCORDION MATERIALS:

Colour Codes:
1 Rowan Wool Cotton
(Shade 00911 – Red) – For Ends
2 Rowan Fine Tweed
(Arncliffe Shade 360 – Oatmeal) – For Bellows
3 Gedifera Samina
(Shade 04321 – Copper) – For Trim

Beads for button keys
Piece of card, enough to cut 2 pairs of rectangles to fit the end sections
Small piece of wadding

NEEDLES:

Size 12/2.75mm
Crochet hook 3.00mm
Darning needle

You will need

JOE BROON MATERIALS:

Colour Codes:
1 Rowan Baby Merino Silk DK
(Shade 674 – Shell Pink) – For Body
2 Sirdar Country Style Wool Blend DK
(Shade 0611 – Caramel) – For Suit
3 Hayfield Bonus DK
(Shade 0947 - Brown) – For Shoes
4 Debbie Bliss Rialto Lace
(Shade 44001 – Cream) – For Shirt
5 Anchor 6 strand embroidery thread 2x hanks
(Shade 373 – Caramel) – For Waistcoat back
6 Anchor 6 strand embroidery thread
(1x Shade 210 – Green and 1x Shade 169 – Blue) – For Tie
7 Debbie Bliss Angel
(Shade 15029 – Gold) – For hair
8 Sublime Baby Cashmerino Silk DK
(Shade 0383 – Yellow)For hair

Beads for jacket buttons, waistcoat, shirt cuffs and eyes
Yarn for creating facial features
Stuffing

NEEDLES:

Size 10/3.25mm
Size 12/2.75mm
Size 12/2.75mm double-ended needles
Size 13/2.25mm
Size 13/2.25mm double-ended needles
Size 14/2mm needles

Crochet hook 1.50mm – for tufts of hair
Crochet hook 3.00mm
Darning needle

Joe
(and his Accordion)

Joe Broon is shorter and stockier than Hen. He and his brother are good pals and they love the outdoors, and their holidays at the But an' Ben. They like a guid party and Joe can contribute to this by playing the bagpipes and the accordion. Like Hen, he served his country during the war. Despite Hen and Joe always being on the look out for a click, they rarely try to be fashionable. They were once seen in duffle coats!

Natty shorts, twinkling feet,
shirt o' navy blue,
Joe Broon knows exactly what
he'd wish to do.
Out on Hampden's velvet turf,
encouraged by the "roar",
Scotland's centre-forward,
scoring goals galore.

BODY

COLOUR I

- Size 10/3.25mm needles

BODY – FRONT

- Cast on 14
- 1st row: K
- 2nd row: P
- 3rd row: K1 inc in next, K10, inc in next, K1 (16sts)
- Work 5 rows SS, starting with P
- 9th row: K1, K2tog, K2, K2tog, K2, K2tog, K2, K2tog, K1 (12sts)
- Work 5 rows SS, starting with P
- 15th row: K2, inc in next, K6, inc in next, K2 (14sts)
- 16th row: P
- 17th row: inc in 1st, K3, inc in next, K4, inc in next, K3, inc in last (18sts)
- 18th row: P
- 19th row: K5, inc in next, K6, inc in next, K5 (20sts)
- 20th row: P
- 21st row: K6, inc in next, K6, inc in next, K6 (22sts)
- 22nd row: P
- 23rd row: K1, sll, K1, psso, K16, K2tog, K1 (20sts)
- Work 5 rows SS, starting with P
- 29th row: K1, sll, K1, psso, K14, K2tog, K1 (18sts)
- 30th row: P1, P2tog, P12, P2tog, P1 (16sts)
- 31st row: K
- 32nd row: P
- Cast off

BODY – BACK

- Cast on 14

- 1st row: K
- 2nd row: P
- 3rd row: K
- 4th row: P
- 5th row: K2, inc in next, K1, inc in next, K4, inc in next, K1, inc in next, K2 (18sts)
- 6th row: P
- 7th row: K3, inc in next, K1, inc in next, K6, inc in next, K1, inc in next, K3 (22sts)
- Work 3 rows SS, starting with P
- 11th row: K1, K2tog, K16, K2tog, K1 (20sts)
- 12th row: P
- 13th row: K2, K2tog, K1, K2tog, K6, K2tog, K1, K2tog, K2 (16sts)
- 14th row: P
- 15th row: K2, K2tog, K2, K2tog, K2tog, K2, K2tog, K2 (12sts)
- Work 5 rows SS, starting with P
- 21st row: K1, inc in next, K3, inc in next, inc in next, K3, inc in next, K1 (16sts)
- Work 7 rows SS, starting with P
- 29th row: K1, inc in next, K12, inc in next, K1 (18sts)
- 30th row: P
- 31st row: K1, sll, K1, psso, K12, K2tog, K1 (16sts)
- 32nd row: P1, P2tog, P10, P2tog, P1 (14sts)
- 33rd row: K
- 34th row: P
- Cast off

To make up: Join front and back. Stuff.

HEAD

COLOUR I

- Size 10/3.25mm needles

RIGHT SIDE OF FACE

- Cast on 5
- 1st row: K
- 2nd row: P
- 3rd row: Cast on 2, K (7sts)
- 4th row: P5, inc in next, inc in next (9sts)
- 5th row: K1, inc in next, inc in next, K6 (11sts)
- 6th row: P11
- Break thread and leave on needle

LEFT SIDE OF FACE WITH WS FACING

- Cast on 5
- 1st row: K
- 2nd row: P
- 3rd row: K to end, cast on 2 (7sts)
- 4th row: P1, inc in next, inc in next, P4 (9sts)
- 5th row: K6, inc in next, inc in next, K1 (11sts)
- 6th row: P11
- Now join 2 pieces together
- 7th row: K10, K2tog, K10 (21sts)
- 8th row: P1, P2tog, P15, P2tog, P1 (19sts)
- Work 6 rows SS, starting with K
- 15th row: K1, sll, K1, psso, K13, K2tog, K1 (17sts)
- 16th row: P
- 17th row: K1, sll, K1, psso, K11, K2tog, K1 (15sts)
- 18th row: P
- 19th row: K1, sll, K1, psso, K9, K2tog, K1 (13sts)
- 20th row: P1, P2tog, P7, P2tog, P1 (11sts)
- 21st row: K1, sll, K1, psso, K5, K2tog, K1 (9sts)
- 22nd row: P
- Cast off

HEAD – BACK

- Cast on 6
- 1st row: K
- 2nd row: P
- 3rd row: K row – inc in 1st and last (8sts)
- 4th row: P
- 5th row: K row – inc in 1st and last (10sts)
- 6th row: P
- 7th row: K row – inc in 1st and last (12sts)
- 8th row: P
- 9th row: K row – inc in 1st and last (14sts)
- Work 7 rows SS, starting with P
- 17th row: K1, sl1, K1, psso, K8, K2tog, K1 (12sts)
- 18th row: P
- 19th row: K1, sl1, K1, psso, K6, K2tog, K1 (10sts)
- 20th row: P
- Cast off

To make up: Join front to back. Stuff.

ARMS – MAKE TWO

COLOUR 1

- Size 10/3.25mm needles
- Size 12/2.75mm double-ended needles

WORKING FROM SHOULDER TO WRIST

- Cast on 5
- 1st row: K
- 2nd row: P
- 3rd row K1, inc in next, K1, inc in next, K1 (7sts)
- 4th row: P
- 5th row: K1, inc in next, K3, inc in next, K1 (9sts)
- 6th row: P
- 7th row: K3, inc in next, K1, inc in next, K3 (11sts)

- 8th row: P
- 9th row: K5, inc in next, K5 (12sts)
- Work 12 rows SS, starting with P
- 22nd row: P2tog, P3, P2tog, P3, P2tog (9sts)
- 23rd row: K2tog, K5, K2tog (7sts)
- 24th row: P
- 25th row: K1, inc in next, K3, inc in next, K1 (9sts)
- 26th row: P
- 27th row: K3, inc in next, K1, inc in next, K3 (11sts)
- Work 3 rows SS, starting with P
- 31st row: K1, K2tog, K5, K2tog, K1 (9sts)
- 32nd row: P
- 33rd row: K
- 34th row: P1, P2tog, P3, P2tog, P1 (7sts)
- 35th row: K
- 36th row: P
- 37th row: K1, K2tog, K1, K2tog, K1 (5sts)
- 38th row: P
- 39th row: K1, inc in next, K1, inc in next, K1 (7sts)
- 40th row: P
- 41st row: K1, inc in next, K3, inc in next, K1 (9sts)
- 42nd row: P

FOR LEFT HAND

- 43rd row: K2, put 2sts on pin, K5 (7sts)
- Work 4 rows SS, starting with P
- 48th row: P2tog, P2tog, P2tog, P1 (4sts)
- 49th row: K2tog, K2tog (2sts)
- Pull wool through

FOR RIGHT HAND

- 43rd row: K5, put 2sts on pin, K2 (7sts)
- Work 4 rows SS, starting with P
- 48th row: P1, P2tog, P2tog, P2tog (4sts)

- 49th row: K2tog, K2tog (2sts)
- Pull wool through

THUMB – SAME FOR BOTH HANDS

- Join wool to 2sts on pin
- Use 12/2.75mm double-ended needles to work i-cord for 3 rows
- Pull wool through and darn end

- To make up: Join seams. Stuff. Attach to body.

LEGS – MAKE TWO

COLOUR 3

- Size 10/3.25mm needles

- Cast on 24
- 1st row: K
- 2nd row: P
- 3rd row: K10, K2tog, K2tog, K10 (22sts)
- 4th row: P10, P2tog, P10 (21sts)
- 5th row: K5, K2tog, K1, K2tog, K1, K2tog, K1, K2tog, K5 (17sts)
- 6th row: P
- 7th row: K4, cast off 8, K4 (9sts)
- 8th row: P 4, P2tog, P3 (8sts)
- Work 4 rows SS, starting with K
- 13th row: K1, inc in next, K4, inc in next, K1 (10sts)
- 14th row: P
- Break thread and JOIN COLOUR 1
- Work 6 rows SS, starting with K
- 21st row: K1, inc in next, K6, inc in next, K1 (12sts)
- Work 7 rows SS, starting with P
- 29th row: K1, inc in next, K8, inc in next, K1 (14sts)
- Work 22 rows SS, starting with P
- Cast off

To make up: Sew-up sole of boot. Stuff boot with offcuts of brown wool rather than white wadding, which tends to show through. Sew leg seams. Attach to body.

SHIRT

COLOUR 4
- Size 13/2.25mm needles
- Size 13/2.25mm double-ended needles

MAIN BODY OF SHIRT
- Cast on 66
- 1st row: K
- 2nd row: K2, P62, K2
- Repeat rows 1 and 2 (x12)
- 27th row: K17, cast off 2, K27, cast off 2, K16 (62sts)

FRONT LEFT SIDE – WITH WS FACING
- Working on 17sts – Put remaining sts on pin
- Work 14 rows SS, starting with P – Each P row starting with K2
- 15th row: Cast off 3, P to end (14sts)
- 16th row: K14
- 17th row: Cast off 2, P to end (12sts)
- 18th row: Cast off 5, K to end (7sts)
- 19th row: P
- Cast off 7
- Pull wool through

BACK – WITH WS FACING
- Working on next 28sts from pin:
- Work 16 rows SS, starting with P
- 17th row: Cast off 11, P16 (17sts)
- 18th row: Cast off 11 and leave remaining 6sts on pin for collar

FRONT RIGHT SIDE – WITH WS FACING
- Working on remaining 17sts
- Work 13 rows SS, starting with P – Each P row ending with K2
- 14th row: Cast off 3, K to end (14sts)
- 15th row: P all sts
- 16th row: Cast off 2, K to end (12sts)
- 17th row: Cast off 5, P to end (7sts)
- 18th row: K
- Cast off

Join shoulder seams.

COLLAR – WITH RS FACING
- Pick up 11sts along right front neck, K6 from pin across back neck, pick up 11sts along left front neck (28sts), turn –
- With WS facing
- 1st row: K
- 2nd row: K1, P26, K1
- 3rd row: K
- 4th row: K1, P26, K1
- 5th row: K1, inc in next, K5, inc in next, K1, inc in next, K8, inc in next, K1, inc in next, K5, inc in next, K1 (34sts)
- 6th row: K1, P32, K1
- 7th row: K
- 8th row: K1, P32, K1
- 9th row: K33, inc in last (35sts)
- Cast off

SLEEVES

LEFT SLEEVE – WORKING FROM SHOULDER TO WRIST
- Cast on 32
- Work 9 rows SS, starting with K
- 10th row: P1, P2tog, P26, P2tog, P1 (30sts)
- Work 9 rows SS, starting with K
- 20th row: P1, P2tog, P24, P2tog, P1 (28sts)
- Work 9 rows SS, starting with K
- 30th row: P1, P2tog, P22, P2tog, P1 (26sts)
- Work 11 rows SS, starting with K
- 42nd row: P1, P2tog, P20, P2tog, P1 (24sts)
- 43rd row: K this row onto 3 double-ended needles
- 44th row: P6, turn –
- 45th row: K6, K18 from other end of needles (this closes the underarm seam and gives a vent opening at the side back), turn –
- 46th row: P
- 47th row: K
- 48th row: P
- 49th row: K3, (K2tog, K2) x2, K2tog, K1, (K2tog) x4, K2 (17sts)
- 50th row: K17, cast on 3 (20sts) – this makes the cuff in reverse SS
- 51st row: K1, P18, K1
- 52nd row: K
- 53rd row: K1, P18, K1
- 54th row: K
- Cast off

RIGHT SLEEVE – WORKING FROM SHOULDER TO WRIST
- Cast on 32
- Work 9 rows SS, starting with K
- 10th row: P1, P2tog, P26, P2tog, P1 (30sts)
- Work 9 rows SS, starting with K
- 20th row: P1, P2tog, P24, P2tog, P1 (28sts)
- Work 9 rows SS, starting with K
- 30th row: P1, P2tog, P22, P2tog, P1 (26sts)
- Work 11 rows SS, starting with K
- 42nd row: P1, P2tog, P20, P2tog, P1 (24sts)
- 43rd row: K this row onto 3 double-ended needles
- 44th row: P18, turn –

- 45th row: K18, K6 from other end of needles (this closes the underarm seam and gives a vent opening at the side back), turn —
- 46th row: P
- 47th row: K
- 48th row: P
- 49th row: K2, (K2tog)x4, K1, K2tog, (K2, K2tog)x2, K3 (17sts)
- 50th row: Cast on 3, knit to end (20sts) – this makes the cuff in reverse SS
- 51st row: K1, P18, K1
- 52nd row: K
- 53rd row: K1, P18, K1
- 54th row: K
- Cast off

To make up: Sew up sleeve seams and inset sleeves. Dress doll and close shirt front. Add cuff buttons. If not wearing jacket, push up sleeves to just above elbow to show brawny forearms. Catch in place with a stitch.

TROUSERS

COLOUR 2
- Size 10/3.25mm needles

RIGHT LEG
- Cast on 19
- Work 45 rows SS, starting with K
- 46th row: P row, inc in 1st and last sts (21sts)
- 47th row: K
- 48th row: Cast off 2, P17 (19sts)
- 49th row: Cast off 2, K15 (17sts)
- 50th row: P
- Hold on a pin

LEFT LEG
- Cast on 19
- Work as right leg to row 50
- Knitting legs together, starting with left leg
- 51st row: K2tog, K14, K last stitch of left leg with first stitch of right leg – K14, K2tog (31sts)
- Work 5 rows SS, starting with P
- 57th row: K6, K2tog, K15, K2tog, K6 (29sts)
- Work 6 rows SS, starting with P
- Cast off

To make up: Join leg and crotch seams. Add to doll.

WAISTCOAT

COLOUR 2
- Size 10/3.25mm needles

RIGHT FRONT
- Cast on 8
- 1st row: K2, turn —
- 2nd row: P1, inc in next (9sts)
- 3rd row: K1, inc in next, K4, turn – (10sts)
- 4th row: P6, inc in next (11sts)
- 5th row: K1, inc in next, K to end (12sts)
- 6th row: P11, K1
- 7th row: K
- 8th row: P11, K1
- 9th row: K
- 10th row: P11, K1
- 11th row: K
- 12th row: P11, K1
- 13th row: K10, inc in next, K1 (13sts)
- 14th row: P12, K1
- 15th row: K
- 16th row: P12, K1
- 17th row: K
- 18th row: P12, K1
- 19th row: K
- 20th row: Cast off 2, P9, K1 (11sts)
- 21st row: K9, K2tog (10sts)
- 22nd row: K1, P2tog, P6, K1 (9sts)
- 23rd row: K1, sl1, K1, psso, K to end (8sts)
- 24th row: K1, P4, P2tog, K1 (7sts)
- 25th row: K1, sl1, K1, psso, K to end (6sts)
- 26th row: K1, P4, K1
- 27th row: K1, sl1, K1, psso, K to end (5sts)
- 28th row: K1, P3, K1
- 29th row: K1, sl1, K1, psso, K to end (4sts)
- 30th row: K1, P2, K1
- 31st row: K1, sl1, K1, psso, K to end (3sts)
- 32nd row: K1, P1, K1
- 33rd row: K
- Cast off

LEFT FRONT
- Cast on 8
- 1st row: P2, turn —
- 2nd row: K1, inc in next (9sts)
- 3rd row: Inc in 1st, P5, turn – (10sts)
- 4th row: K5, inc in next, K1 (11sts)
- 5th row: Inc in 1st, P to end (12sts)
- 6th row: K
- 7th row: K1, P to end
- 8th row: K
- 9th row: K1, P to end
- 10th row: K
- 11th row: K1, P to end
- 12th row: K
- 13th row: K1, P to end
- 14th row: K1, inc in next, K to end (13sts)
- 15th row: K1, P to end
- 16th row: K
- 17th row: K1, P to end
- 18th row: K

- 19th row: K1, P to end
- 20th row: Cast off 2, K to end (11sts)
- 21st row: K1, P8, P2tog (10sts)
- 22nd row: K2tog, K to end (9sts)
- 23rd row: K1, P2tog, P5, K1 (8sts)
- 24th row: K5, K2tog, K1 (7sts)
- 25th row: K1, P2tog, P3, K1 (6sts)
- 26th row: K
- 27th row: K1, P2tog, P2, K1 (5sts)
- 28th row: K
- 29th row: K1, P2tog, P1, K1 (4sts)
- 30th row: K
- 31st row: K1, P2tog, K1 (3sts)
- 32nd row: K
- 33rd row: K1, P1, K1
- Cast off

BACK
COLOUR 5
- Size 14/2mm needles

- Cast on 24
- Work 8 rows SS, starting with K
- 9th row: K1, K2tog, K8, K2tog, K8, K2tog, K1 (21sts)
- Work 5 rows SS, starting with P
- 15th row: K10, inc in next, K10 (22sts)
- 16th row: P
- 17th row: K10, inc in next, inc in next, K10 (24sts)
- Work 4 rows SS, starting with P
- 22nd row: Cast off 2, P to end (22sts)
- 23rd row: Cast off 2, K to end (20sts)
- 24th row: P2tog, P16, P2tog (18sts)
- Work 12 rows SS, starting with K
- 37th row: K6, turn –
- 38th row: P6
- 39th row: K5, turn –

- 40th row: P5
- 41st row: Cast off 5, K to end (13sts)
- 42nd row: P6, turn –
- 43rd row: K6
- 44th row: P5, turn –
- 45th row: K5
- Cast off all sts

To make up: Join front to back at side seams and shoulder seams. Dress doll. Join at centre front and add beads for buttons.

JACKET
COLOUR 2
- Size 10/3.25mm needles

FRONT AND BACK – LEFT
- Cast on 24
- 1st row: K
- 2nd row: K1, P22, K1
- 3rd row: K
- 4th row: K1, P22, K1
- 5th row: K
- 6th row: K1, P22, K1
- 7th row: K
- 8th row: K1, P22, K1
- 9th row: K
- 10th row: K1, P22, K1
- 11th row: K11, K2tog, K11 (23sts)
- 12th row: K1, P21, K1
- Break thread, set aside on a pin

FRONT AND BACK – RIGHT
- Cast on 26
- 1st row: K
- 2nd row: K1, P24, K1
- 3rd row: K
- 4th row: K1, P24, K1

- 5th row: K
- 6th row: K1, P24, K1
- 7th row: K
- 8th row: K1, P24, K1
- 9th row: K
- 10th row: K1, P24, K1
- 11th row: K11, K2tog, K13 (25sts)
- 12th row: Cast off 2, P21, K1 (23sts)

TO JOIN JACKET PIECES TOGETHER
- With RS facing, work row 13 across front and back right, followed by front and back left
- 13th row: K22, K last stitch from right side and first from left side together, K22 (45sts)
- 14th row: K1, P43, K1
- 15th row: K
- 16th row: K1, P43, K1
- 17th row: K13, K2tog, K15, K2tog, K13 (43sts)

- 18th row: K1, P41, K1
- 19th row: K
- 20th row: K1, P41, K1
- 21st row: K
- 22nd row: K1, P41, K1
- 23rd row: K13, inc in next, K15, inc in next, K13 (45sts)
- 24th row: K1, P43, K1
- 25th row: K11, inc in next, K21, inc in next, K11 (47sts)
- 26th row: K1, P45, K1
- 27th row: K1, inc in next, K43, inc in next, K1 (49sts)
- 28th row: K2, P45, K2
- 29th row: K1, P1, K45, P1, K1
- 30th row: K3, P10, cast off 2, P18, cast off 2, P9, K3 (45sts)

WORKING ON RIGHT FRONT (13STS)
- 31st row: K1, P2, K8, K2tog (12sts)
- 32nd row: P9, K3
- 33rd row: K1, P3, K8
- 34th row: P8, K4
- 35th row: K1, P3, K8
- 36th row: P7, K5
- 37th row: K1, P4, K7
- 38th row: P7, K5
- 39th row: Cast off 3, P1, K7 (9sts)
- 40th row: P7, put last 2 sts on pin for collar, turn –
- 41st row: K7
- 42nd row: Cast off 3, P3 (4sts)
- 43rd row: Cast off 4

WORKING ON JACKET BACK – NEXT 19 STS – RS FACING
- Work 10 rows SS, starting with K
- 41st row: Cast off 3, K15 (16sts)

- 42nd row: Cast off 3, P12 (13sts)
- 43rd row: Cast off 3, K9 (10sts)
- 44th row: Cast off 3, put remaining 7 sts on pin for collar

WORKING ON FRONT LEFT – REMAINING 13 STS – RS FACING
- 31st row: K2tog, K8, P2, K1 (12sts)
- 32nd row: K3, P9
- 33rd row: K8, P3, K1
- 34th row: K4, P8
- 35th row: K8, P3, K1
- 36th row: K5, P7
- 37th row: K7, P4, K1
- 38th row: K5, P7
- 39th row: K7, P4, K1
- 40th row: Cast off 3, K1, P7 (9sts)
- 41st row: K7, put last 2 sts on pin for collar, turn –
- 42nd row: P7
- 43rd row: K7
- 44th row: P7
- 45th row: Cast off 3, K3 (4sts)
- 46th row: Cast off 4

To make up: Join shoulder seams. Catch top of centre back vent.

UPPER COLLAR
- Size 12/2.75mm

WORKING WITH WS FACING
- 1st row: K2 sts from left lapel, pick up 6 sts along left front neck, K7 from back neck, pick up 6 sts along right front neck, K2 sts from right lapel (23sts)
- 2nd row: K1, P21, K1
- 3rd row: K

- 4th row: K1, inc in next, P19, inc in next, K1 (25sts)
- 5th row: K9, inc in next, K5, inc in next, K8, inc in last (28sts)
- Cast off loosely

To make up: Steam press to tidy collar and lapels.

JACKET SLEEVES – MAKE TWO
- Cast on 14
- Work 11 rows SS, starting with K
- 12th row: P row, inc in 1st and last st (16sts)
- Work 6 rows SS, starting with K
- 19th row: For left sleeve, K3, inc in next, K12 (17sts) For right sleeve, K11, inc in next, K4 (17sts)
- Work 12 rows SS, starting with P
- 32nd row: Cast off 2, P to end (15sts)
- 33rd row: Cast off 2, K to end (13sts)
- 34th row: P2tog, P9, P2tog (11sts)
- Work 4 rows SS, starting with K
- 39th row: K2tog, K7, K2tog (9sts)
- 40th row: P2tog, P5, P2tog (7sts)
- 41st row: K
- Cast off

SHOULDER PADS – MAKE TWO
- Cast on 8
- Work 9 rows SS
- Cast off

To make up: Join seams. Inset to jacket. Fold shoulder pads in half diagonally and catch stitch inside jacket. To finish the suit dress doll and add beads as front and cuff buttons.

TIE

COLOUR 6 – combining 4 strand green and 2 strands blue
- Size 12/2.75mm needles

- Cast on 7
- Work 22 rows SS, starting with K
- 23rd row: K3, K2tog, K2 (6sts)
- Work 3 rows SS, starting with P
- 27th row: K2, K2tog, K2 (5sts)
- Work 12 rows SS, starting with P
- 40th row: K2, K2tog, K1 (4sts)
- Work SS, starting with P until work measures 21cm long
- Cast off

To make up: Steam press flat, fold wide end into point and stitch into place. Place around neck so that it lies under collar. Wrap narrow end around twice to form knot and secure with stitch.

HAIR

COLOUR 7 for base and 7 and 8 for longer hair on crown – COLOUR 8 PARE DOWN A SMALL AMOUNT TO SINGLE STRANDS
- Size 10/3.25mm needles

- Cast on 14
- 1st row: K
- 2nd row: P
- 3rd row: K
- 4th row: P
- 5th row: K1, inc in next, K10, inc in next, K1 (16sts)
- 6th row: P
- 7th row: K
- 8th row: P
- 9th row: K1, inc in next, K12, inc in next, K1 (18sts)
- 10th row: P
- 11th row: K
- 12th row: P14, turn –
- 13th row: K10, turn –
- 14th row: P14 (18sts)
- 15th row: K5, K2tog, K4, K2tog, K5 (16sts)
- 16th row: P2tog, P10, turn –
- 17th row: K8, turn –
- 18th row: P10, P2tog (14sts)
- 19th row: K12, turn –
- 20th row: P10, turn –
- 21st row: K12 (14sts)
- 22nd row: P2tog, P10, P2tog (12sts)
- 23rd row: K2tog, K2, K2tog, K2tog, K2, K2tog (8sts)
- 24th row: P
- Cast off loosely

COLOUR 8
- Size 10/3.25 needles

- Knit a square of 11 rows of 9 sts

To make up: To square up the crown and add height, position and attach small knitted square to crown. Stitch hairpiece over this from centre front hairline to nape of neck after positioning ears (see TO CREATE FACE). Using the 1.5mm crochet hook or a darning needle, insert and knot in lengths of COLOUR 7 and 8 until the crown is covered. Chop short to stand up.

Tip: Make crown hair longer than finished length and cut short with hairdressing scissors.

TO CREATE FACE

The nose and ears are crocheted chains in flesh colour. Stitch to shape and add to head and face. Use own choice of wool for brows and mouth. Add beads for eyes.
Refer to a cartoon to capture the essence of handsome Joe.

Joe (and his Accordion)

Button Accordion

FINGER PLATES/ENDS – MAKE TWO

COLOUR 1

- Size 12/2.75mm needles

- Cast on 19
- Work 9 rows SS, starting with K – on each P row K 1st and last st
- Cast off

MAIN BODY/BELLOWS

- COLOURS 1, 2 and 3
- Size 12/2.75mm needles

- Cast on 38
- 1st row: K
- 2nd row: P
- 3rd row: K
- 4th row: K
- 5th row: Join in COLOUR 2, K
- 6th row: K1, P36, K1
- 7th row: K13, sl1, K1, psso, K2tog, K4, sl1, K1, psso, K2tog, K13 (34sts)
- 8th row: K1, P11, P2tog, P2tog, P2, P2tog, P2tog, P11, K1 (30sts)
- 9th row: K
- 10th row: K1, P28, K1
- 11th row: K12, inc in next, inc in next, K2, inc in next, inc in next, K12 (34sts)
- 12th row: K1, P12, inc in next, inc in next, P4, inc in next, inc in next, P12, K1 (38sts)
- 13th row: Join in COLOUR 3, K
- 14th row: K
- 15th row: Join in COLOUR 2, K
- Repeat from row 6 to row 15 seven times more
- 86th row: K1, P36, K1
- 87th row: K13, sl1, K1, psso, K2tog, K4, sl1, K1, psso, K2tog, K13 (34sts)
- 88th row: K1, P11, P2tog, P2tog, P2, P2tog, P2tog, P11, K1 (30sts)
- 89th row: K
- 90th row: K1, P28, K1
- 91st row: K12, inc in next, inc in next, K2, inc in next, inc in next, K12 (34sts)
- 92nd row: K1, P12, inc in next, inc in next, P4, inc in next, inc in next, P12, K1 (38sts)
- 93rd row: Join in COLOUR 1, K
- 94th row: K
- 95th row: K
- 96th row: P
- 97th row: K
- Cast off

To make up: Concertina up the bellows sections. Steam press in place. Fold in half and sew side edges of the work together – this is the bottom of the instrument. Stitch firmly and closely together which allows the top to fan open. Sew the end pieces in place – these will be about 1cm longer to allow them to fold under the bottom edge. Before sewing around the bottom, insert the two pairs of card cut to size with wadding sandwiched between each to create the box shape for the end sections. Sew rows of beads to look like accordion buttons on the ends. Work a length of crochet chain to make a strap at each end and sew in place. Give to Joe and get your dancing shoes on!

You will need

MATERIALS:

Colour Codes:
1 Rowan Baby Merino DK
(Shade 674 – Shell Pink) – For Body
2 Debbie Bliss Rialto Lace
(Shade 44018 – Blue) – For Dress
3 Debbie Bliss Rialto Lace
(Shade 44026 – Coral) – For Cardigan
5 Rowan Cotton Glace
(Shade 843 – Rich Brown) – For Sandals
6 Rowan Baby Merino Silk DK
(Shade – 671 – Straw) – For Hair
7 Skein of yellow/cream-coloured embroidery
thread pared down to single strands

Beads for eyes and cardigan
Yarn for creating facial features
Stuffing

NEEDLES:
Size 11/3.0
Size 12/2.75mm double-ended
Size 13/2.75mm
Size 14/2.00mm
Crochet hook – 3.00mm
Crochet hook – 1.5mm
Darning needle

Maggie windae shoppin

Maggie

Maggie Broon is the stylish, glamorous one. Never seen without her lipstick, even at the tattie howkin'. Since 1936, she and her sister Daphne have always tried to keep up with current fashions and hairstyles. She and Daphne get on very well. There were never such devoted sisters . . . unless in competition for an eligible bachelor. In 1977, she was engaged to Dave McKay. Whatever happened to him? None of the other Broons offspring have come as close to marriage.

Maggie's real ambitious, here is what she thinks –
"Oh, to be a film star, decked out wi' jewels an' minks. Posing for the camera like the glamorous heroines. Idol o' the picters, frae 'bobs', tae 'four-and-nines'."

BODY

COLOUR 1
- Size 11/3.00mm needles

BODY – FRONT
- Cast on 14
- 1st row: K
- 2nd row: P
- 3rd row: K2, inc in next, K8, inc in next, K2 (16sts)
- 4th row: P
- 5th row: K
- 6th row: P1, (P2tog, P2)x3, P2tog, P1 (12sts)
- 7th row: K
- 8th row: P
- 9th row: K2tog, K8, K2tog (10sts)
- 10th row: P2tog, P6, P2tog (8sts)
- Work 4 rows SS, starting with K
- 15th row: K2, inc in next, K2, inc in next, K2 (10sts)
- 16th row: P
- 17th row: K1, inc in next, K6, inc in next, K1 (12sts)
- 18th row: P
- 19th row: K1, (inc in next, K2)x3, inc in next, K1 (16sts)
- Work 6 rows SS, starting with P
- 26th row: P1, P2tog, P10, P2tog, P1 (14sts)
- 27th row: K
- 28th row: P
- 29th row: K1, sl1, K1, psso, K8, K2tog, K1 (12sts)
- 30th row: P
- Cast off

BODY – BACK
- Cast on 16
- 1st row: K

- 2nd row: P
- 3rd row: K3, (inc in next, K2)x3, inc in next, K3 (20sts)
- 4th row: P16, turn –
- 5th row: K12, turn –
- 6th row: P16
- 7th row: K1, K2tog, K3, K2tog, K4, K2tog, K3, K2tog, K1 (16sts)
- 8th row: P1, P2tog, P8, turn –
- 9th row: K6, turn –
- 10th row: P8, P2tog, P1 (14sts)
- 11th row: K1, K2tog, K2, K2tog, K2tog, K2, K2tog, K1 (10sts)
- Work 5 rows SS, starting with P
- 17th row: K1, inc in next, K6, inc in next, K1 (12sts)
- 18th row: P
- 19th row: K4, inc in next, K2, inc in next, K4 (14sts)
- Work 5 rows SS, starting with P
- 25th row: K1, inc in next, K10, inc in next, K1 (16sts)
- 26th row: P
- 27th row: K1, inc in next, K12, inc in next, K1 (18sts)
- 28th row: P
- 29th row: K1, sl1, K1, psso, K12, K2tog, K1 (16sts)
- 30th row: P
- 31st row: K1, sl1, K1, psso, K10, K2tog, K1 (14sts)
- 32nd row: P
- Cast off

BUST – MAKE TWO
COLOUR 1
- Size 11/3.00mm needles

- Cast on 15
- 1st row: K
- 2nd row: (P1, P2tog)x5 (10sts)
- 3rd row: K2tog, K1, K2tog, K2tog, K1, K2tog, (6sts)
- Break wool and pull through 5sts, tie off

To make up: Sew-up sides. Place over a bead or marble and steam to shape. Stuff.

ARMS – MAKE TWO

COLOUR 1
- Size 11/3.00mm needles

WORKING FROM SHOULDER TO WRIST
- Cast on 4
- 1st row: K
- 2nd row: P
- 3rd row: K row – inc in 1st and last (6sts)
- 4th row: P
- 5th row: K row – inc in 1st and last (8sts)
- Work 13 rows SS, starting with P
- 19th row: K2tog, K4, K2tog (6sts)
- 20th row: P
- 21st row: K2, inc in next, inc in next, K2 (8sts)
- Work 3 rows SS, starting with P
- 25th row: K3, K2tog, K3 (7sts)
- 26th row: P
- 27th row: K
- 28th row: P2tog, P3, P2tog (5sts)
- Work 4 rows SS, starting with K
- 33rd row: K row – inc in 1st, K1, inc in next, K1, inc in last (8sts)

FOR LEFT HAND
- 34th row: P4, inc in next, P3 (9sts)
- 35th row: K2, put 2 on pin, K5

- Work 3 rows SS, starting with P
- 39th row: K2tog, K2tog, K2tog, K1 (4sts)
- 40th row: P2tog, P2tog
- Pull wool through

FOR RIGHT HAND

- 34th row: P3, inc in next, P4 (9sts)
- 35th row: K5, put 2 on pin, K2
- Work 3 rows SS, starting with P
- 39th row: K1, K2tog, K2tog, K2tog (4sts)
- 40th row: P2tog, P2tog
- Pull wool through

THUMBS – SAME FOR BOTH HANDS

- Put 2sts from pin on size 12/2.75mm double-ended needle
- Join thread – K2, K2tog as i-cord
- Pull wool through

To make up: Join seams. Stuff. Attach to body.

HEAD

COLOUR 1

- Size 11/3.00mm needles

FRONT-RIGHT OF FACE

- Cast on 3
- Work 4 rows SS, starting with K
- 5th row: Cast on 3, K to end (6sts)
- 6th row: P row, inc in 1st, P5 (7sts)
- Break wool, hold sts on left-hand needle

FRONT-LEFT OF FACE

- Cast on 3 on same needle
- Now, working on these 3sts only:
- Work 5 rows SS, starting with K
- 6th row: Cast on 3, P6, inc in last (7sts)

- 7th row: Work across 2 pieces – K6, K2tog, K6 (13sts)
- 8th row: P
- 9th row: K row – inc in 1st and last (15sts)
- Work 3 rows SS, starting with P
- 13th row: K row – inc in 1st and last (17sts)
- Work 3 rows SS, starting with P
- 17th row: K2tog, K13, K2tog (15sts)
- 18th row: P
- 19th row: K2tog, K11, K2tog (13sts)
- 20th row: P
- 21st row: K2tog, K9, K2tog (11sts)
- 22nd row: P
- 23rd row: K2tog, K7, K2tog (9sts)
- 24th row: P
- Cast off

HEAD – BACK

- Cast on 3
- Work 4 rows SS, starting with K
- 5th row: K – inc in 1st and last (5sts)
- 6th row: P
- 7th row: K – inc in 1st and last (7sts)
- 8th row: P
- 9th row: K – inc in 1st and last (9sts)
- 10th row: P
- 11th row: K – inc in 1st and last (11sts)
- 12th row: P
- 13th row: K1, inc in next, K2, inc in next, K1, inc in next, K2, inc in next, K1 (15sts)
- Work 7 rows SS, starting with P
- 21st row: K2tog, K3, K2tog, K1, K2tog, K3, K2tog (11sts)
- 22nd row: P
- 23rd row: K2tog, K7, K2tog (9sts)
- 25th row: P
- Cast off

To make up: Join front to back. Stuff.

LEGS – MAKE TWO

COLOUR 1

- Size 11/3.00mm needles
- Cast on 4
- 1st row: K
- 2nd row: P
- 3rd row: K1, inc in next, inc in next, K1 (6sts)
- 4th row: P
- 5th row: K1, inc in next, K2, inc in next, K1 (8sts)
- 6th row: P
- 7th row: K1, inc in next, K1, inc in next, inc in next, K1, inc in next, K1 (12sts)
- 8th row: P2tog, P8, P2tog (10sts)
- 9th row: K2tog, K6, K2tog (8sts)
- Work 3 rows SS, starting with P
- 13th row: Cast on 2, K10
- 14th row: Cast on 2, P12
- 15th row: K2tog, K2, K2tog, K2tog, K2, K2tog (8sts)
- 16th row: P
- 17th row: K2tog, K4, K2tog (6sts)
- 18th row: P2, P2tog, P2 (5sts)
- Work 6 rows SS, starting with K
- 25th row: K1, inc in next, K1, inc in next, K1 (7sts)
- 26th row: P
- 27th row: K
- 28th row: P1, inc in next, P3, inc in next, P1 (9sts)
- 29th row: K
- 30th row: P
- 31st row: K1, inc in next, K5, inc in next, K1 (11sts)
- Work 6 rows SS, starting with P

- 38th row: P1, P2tog, P5, P2tog, P1 (9sts)
- 39th row: K1, sl1, K1, psso, K3, K2tog, K1 (7sts)
- Work 3 rows SS, starting with P
- 43rd row: K1, inc in next, K3, inc in next, K1 (9sts)
- Work 4 rows SS, starting with P
- 48th row: P1, inc in next, P5, inc in next, P1 (11sts)
- Work 3 rows SS, starting with K
- 52nd row: P1, inc in next, P7, inc in next, P1 (13sts)
- Work 5 rows SS, starting with K
- 58th row: P1, inc in next, P9, inc in next, P1 (15sts)
- Work 3 rows SS, starting with K
- 62nd row: P1, inc in next, P12, inc in next, P1 (17sts)
- 63rd row: K
- Cast off

To make up: Stitch seam under foot to heel and stuff foot. Working a few stitches at a time, close leg seam stuffing the leg as you go. Attach to body.

DRESS

COLOUR 2
- Size 14/2.00mm needles

DRESS – FRONT
- Cast on 66
- Work 4 rows SS, starting with K
- 5th row: K2, (K3, K2tog)x6, K2, (K2tog, K3)x6, K2 (54sts)
- Work 13 rows SS, starting with P
- 19th row: K4, (K2tog, K3)x4, K2tog, K2, (K2tog, K3)x4, K2tog, K4 (44sts)

- Work 13 rows SS, starting with P
- 33rd row: K3, (K2tog, K2)x9, K2tog, K3 (34sts)
- Work 13 rows SS, starting with P
- 47th row: K3, (K2tog, K2)x3, K2tog, K2tog, (K2, K2tog)x3, K3 (26sts)
- Work 7 rows SS, starting with P
- 55th row: K3, K2tog, K16, K2tog, K3 (24sts)
- Work 2 rows SS, starting with P
- 58th row: P6, P2tog, P8, P2tog, P6 (22sts)
- Work 4 rows SS, starting with K
- 63rd row: K2, inc in next, K4, inc in next, K6, inc in next, K4, inc in next, K2 (26sts)
- Work 3 rows SS, starting with P
- 67th row: K2, inc in next, K5, inc in next, K8, inc in next, K5 inc in next, K2 (30sts)
- Work 4 rows SS, starting with P
- 72nd row: K
- 73rd row: K24, turn –
- 74th row: P18, turn –
- 75th row: K17, K2tog, K5
- 76th row: P22, P2tog, P5 (28sts)
- 77th row: K
- 78th row: K2tog, K24, K2tog (26sts)
- Cast off working first 2 and last 2 sts together

DRESS – BACK
- Cast on 62
- Work 4 rows SS, starting with K
- 5th row: (K3, K2tog)x6, K2, (K2tog, K3)x6 (50sts)
- Work 13 rows SS, starting with P
- 19th row: K2, (K2tog, K3)x4, K2tog, K2, (K2tog, K3)x4, K2tog, K2 (40sts)
- Work 13 rows SS, starting with P
- 33rd row: K1, (K2tog, K2)x9, K2tog, K1 (30sts)

- Work 13 rows SS, starting with P
- 47th row: K1, (K2tog, K2)x3, K2tog, K2tog, (K2, K2tog)x3, K1 (22sts)
- Work 7 rows SS, starting with P
- 55th row: K1, K2tog, K16, K2tog, K1 (20sts)
- Work 2 rows SS, starting with P
- 58th row: P5, P2tog, P6, P2tog, P5 (18sts)
- Work 4 rows SS, starting with K
- 63rd row: K row, inc in 1st, K4, inc in next, K6, inc in next, K4, inc in last (22sts)
- Work 3 rows SS, starting with P
- 67th row: K row, inc in 1st, K5, inc in next, K8, inc in next, K5, inc in last (26sts)
- Work 13 rows SS, starting with P
- Cast off

To make up: Steam press both pieces under a damp cloth. Join one side seam. Dress doll, pin and close second seam.

CARDIGAN

COLOUR 3
- Size 14/2.00mm needles

- Cast on 56
- Work 5 rows 1 and 1 rib
- 6th row: K
- 7th row: K2, P52, K2
- Repeat rows 6 and 7 eight more times
- 24th row: K
- 25th row: K2, P11, cast off 2, P25, cast off 2, P10, K2 (52sts)
- Working on 13 sts for right front:
- 26th row: K
- 27th row: P11, K2
- Repeat rows 26 and 27 five more times
- 38th row: Cast off 3, K7, K2tog (9sts)
- 39th row: P7, K2tog (8sts)

- 40th row: K2tog, K6 (7sts)
- Cast off
- Working on the next 26 sts with RS facing:
- Work 12 rows SS, starting with K
- 38th row: K7, turn –
- 39th row: P7
- 40th row: K6, K2tog, K18 (25sts)
- 41st row: P7
- 42nd row: K7
- Cast off, working the 7th and 8th sts together
- WORKING ON REMAINING 13 STS FOR LEFT FRONT WITH RS FACING:
- 26th row: K
- 27th row: K2, P11
- Repeat rows 26 and 27 four more times
- 36th row: K
- 37th row: Cast off 3, P7, P2tog (9sts)
- 38th row: K7, K2tog (8sts)
- 39th row: K2tog, P6 (7sts)
- 40th row: K
- Cast off

SLEEVES – MAKE TWO
COLOUR 3
- Size 14/2.00mm needles

- Cast on 24
- Work 4 rows 1 and 1 rib
- Work 12 rows SS, starting with K
- 17th row: K1, inc in next, K20, inc in next, K1 (26sts)
- Work 9 rows SS, starting with P
- 27th row: K1, inc in next, K22, inc in next, K1 (28sts)
- Work 4 rows SS, starting with P
- 32nd row: Cast off 2, P to end (26sts)
- 33rd row: Cast off 2, K to end (24sts)

- 34th row: P
- 35th row: K2tog, K18, turn –
- 36th row: P16, turn –
- 37th row: K15, K2tog, K1, K2tog
- 38th row: P17, P2tog, P2 (20sts)
- 39th row: K16, turn –
- 40th row: P12, turn –
- 41st row: K11, K2tog, K3
- 42nd row: P14, P2tog, P3 (18sts)
- 43rd row: K
- Cast off

To make up: Press under damp cloth. Join seams. Inset in cardigan.
Dress doll. Add beads as buttons on cardigan front.

HAIR
COLOUR 6 and COLOUR 7

Tip: Add nose and ears before hair. See TO CREATE FACE.

Cut 75cm lengths of both yarns. Working with one length of yarn and two lengths of embroidery thread at a time, fold the lengths over on themselves a few times to form small skeins measuring approx. 18cm in length. Secure these in the middle. Stitch skeins to head to form hairstyle with centre parting. Work from front of hairline to back of head. For added fullness, make up some shorter hanks and attach a few at the back of the head in a line at ear level and again below. Use the crochet hook to hook in and tie a few single strands of COLOUR 7 around the hairline at the front. Roll the bottom of each skein around a pencil to form curls at shoulder level. Slip pencil out and secure curls with a few stitches.

TO CREATE FACE

For nose, crochet a chain using 3.00mm hook. Fold in half, stitch together and add to face. The ears are two crocheted chains coiled round and stitched to shape.

Using a fine yarn and colour of your choice, add mouth and eyebrows.
Add beads for eyes

SANDALS – MAKE TWO
COLOUR 5
- Size 12/2.75mm needles

- Cast on 8
- 1st row: K
- 2nd row: P
- 3rd row: Cast off 1, K6 (7sts)
- 4th row: Cast off 1, P5 (6sts)
- 5th row: K2tog, K2, K2tog (4sts)
- 6th row: P1, P2tog, P1 (3sts)
- Continue in SS for 4 rows starting with K
- 11th row: K1, inc in next, K1 (4sts)
- Work 9 rows SS, starting with P
- 21st row: K2tog, K2tog (2sts)
- Cast off

To make up: Rows 1-5 form the heel of the sandal. Roll this end of the knitted piece round and stitch to form a tubular heel. fold down and secure to the sides of the sole. Stuff with an offcut of COLOUR 5 yarn and close heel at the bottom.

SANDAL STRAPS – MAKE 2 PAIRS

- Cast on 8
- K one row
- Cast off

To make up: Place over foot and attach to sole to form straps of sandal.

Daphne can't resist

You will need

MATERIALS:

Colour Codes:
1 Rowan Baby Merino Silk DK
(Shade 674 – Shell Pink) – For Body
2 Debbie Bliss Baby Cashmerino
(Shade 340068 – Flesh) – For Legs
3 Debbie Bliss Baby Cashmerino
(Shade 340011 – DK Brown) – For Shoes,
Cardigan and Hair
4 Rowan Felted Tweed
(Shade 182 – Heather) – For Skirt
5 Rowan Pure Wool 4ply
(Shade 00465 – Dusky Pink) – For Jumper
6 Gedifera Aneja (Shade 01121 – Bronze) –
For Handbag
7 Hank of black embroidery thread – For Hair

Beads for jacket buttons and eyes
2 bronze-coloured beads for bag fastener
Yarn for creating facial features
Reel of brown thread
Small piece of card for gusset of bag
Stuffing

NEEDLES:

Size 10/3.25m
Size 11/3.00mm
Size 12/2.75mm
Size 12/2.75mm double-ended
Crochet hook 3.5mm
Crochet hook 3.00mm
Darning needle

Daphne

Though plump and less glamorous than her sister Maggie, Daphne Broon does her best to get dolled up and has had her share of lumbers (none of them oil paintings, though). Her diets receive no support from the family, and she's the butt of many a joke. When a letter or package arrives to 'Miss Broon', confusion reigns (though you can bet it's probably meant for the Bairn). Unlike the other Broons, Maggie and Daphne have had varied hairstyles over the years. You can often tell what decade it is from Daphne's hairdo.

Bonny face, silky hair,
trim and slender shape,
Daphne, if she could,
would make the fellows gape.
All the handsome lads wid be
run richt aff their feet,
tryin' to date the Pin-Up,
from No. 10 Glebe Street.

BODY

COLOUR 1

- Size 10/3.25mm needles

BODY – FRONT

- Cast on 16
- 1st row: K
- 2nd row: P
- 3rd row: K1, inc in next, K12, inc in next, K1 (18sts)
- Work 3 rows SS, starting with P
- 7th row: K1, K2tog, K2, K2tog, K4, K2tog, K2, K2tog, K1 (14sts)
- Work 3 rows SS, starting with P
- 11th row: K2, inc in next, K8, inc in next, K2 (16sts)
- 12th row: P
- 13th row: K row – inc in 1st, K3, inc in next, K6, inc in next, K3, inc in last (20sts)
- Work 5 rows SS, starting with P
- 19th row: K1, sl1, K1, psso, inc in next, K12, inc in next, K2tog, K1 (20sts)
- Work 3 rows SS, starting with P
- 23rd row: K1, sl1, K1, psso, K14, K2tog, K1 (18sts)
- 24th row: P2tog, P14, P2tog (16sts)
- 25th row: K1, sl1, K1, psso, K10, K2tog, K1 (14sts)
- 26th row: P
- 27th row: K1, sl1, K1 psso, K8, K2tog, K1 (12sts)
- Cast off

BODY – BACK

- Cast on 16
- 1st row: K
- 2nd row: P
- 3rd row: K2, inc in next, K1, inc in next, K6, inc in next, K1, inc in next, K2 (20sts)
- 4th row: P
- 5th row: K3, inc in next, K1, inc in next, K8, inc in next, K1, inc in next, K3 (24sts)
- Work 3 rows SS, starting with P
- 9th row: K1, K2tog, K18, K2tog, K1 (22sts)
- 10th row: P
- 11th row: K2, K2tog, K1, K2tog, K8, K2tog, K1, K2tog, K2 (18sts)
- 12th row: P
- 13th row: (K2, K2tog)x4, K2 (14sts)
- Work 5 rows SS, starting with P
- 19th row: K1, inc in next, K4, inc in next, inc in next, K4, inc in next, K1 (18sts)
- Work 5 rows SS, starting with P
- 25th row: K1, sl1, K1, psso, K12, K2tog, K1 (16sts)
- 26th row: P
- 27th row: K1, sl1, K1, psso, K10, K2tog, K1 (14sts)
- 28th row: P
- 29th row: K1, sl1, K1, psso, K8, K2tog, K1 (12sts)
- Cast off

To make up: Join two pieces together. Stuff but do not overstuff.

UPPER TORSO/BUST – MAKE TWO

COLOUR 1

- Size 10/3.25mm needles

- Cast on 10
- 1st row: K
- 2nd row: P2tog, P6, P2tog (8sts)
- 3rd row: K2tog, K4, K2tog (6sts)
- 4th row: P2tog, P2, P2tog (4sts)
- 5th row: K
- Cast off
- The cast-on edge is the base of the triangles

CENTRAL BUST PANEL – MAKE ONE

COLOUR 1

- Size 10/3.25mm needles
-
- Cast on 10
- 1st row: K
- 2nd row: P2tog, P6, P2tog (8sts)
- 3rd row: K2tog, K4, K2tog (6sts)
- 4th row: P2tog, P2, P2tog (4sts)
- 5th row: K
- Cast off
- The cast-on edge is the base of the triangles

CENTRAL BUST PANEL – MAKE ONE

COLOUR 1

- Size 10/3.25mm needles
-
- Cast on 14
- 1st row: K
- 2nd row: P
- 3rd row: K2tog, K10, K2tog (12sts)
- 4th row: P
- 5th row: K2tog, K8, K2tog (10sts)
- 6th row: P
- 7th row: K2tog, K6, K2tog (8sts)
- 8th row: P
- 9th row: K
- 10th row: P row – inc in 1st and last (10sts)
- 11th row: K
- 12th row: P row – inc in 1st and last (12sts)
- 13th row: K
- 14th row: P row – inc in 1st and last (14sts)

- 15th row: K
- Cast off

To make up: Stitch each triangle to either end of the central bust panel to form a 'tent' shape. Attach to upper torso of body shape, leaving a small gap to push stuffing through. When happy with shape, sew-up the gap.

ARMS – MAKE TWO

COLOUR I
- Size 10/3.25mm needles

WORKING FROM SHOULDER TO WRIST
- Cast on 5
- 1st row: K
- 2nd row: P
- 3rd row: K row – inc in 1st and last (7sts)
- 4th row: P
- 5th row: K row – inc in 1st and last (9sts)
- 6th row: P
- Work 22 rows

TO CREATE LEFT HAND
- 31st row: K2, put 2 on pin, K5
- 32nd row: P to end bringing 2 sections together (7sts)
- 33rd row: K
- 34th row: P2tog, P2tog, P2tog, P1
- 35th row: K2tog, K2tog
- Pull thread through

TO CREATE RIGHT HAND
- 31st row: K5, put 2 on pin, K2 (7sts)
- 32nd row: P
- 33rd row: K
- 34th row: P1, P2tog, P2tog, P2tog
- 35th row: K2tog, KP2tog

- Pull thread through

THUMB – SAME FOR BOTH HANDS
- Put 2sts from pin on size 12/2.75mm double-ended needle
- Join thread, K2
- K2tog as i-cord
- Pull thread through

To make up: Join seams. Stuff. Attach to body.

LEGS – MAKE TWO

COLOUR 2
- Size 10/3.25mm needles

- Cast on 18
- 1st row: K6, K2tog, K2, K2tog, K6 (16sts)
- 2nd row: P7, P2tog, P7 (15sts)
- 3rd row: K
- 4th row:
  Left leg: P2tog, P5, P2tog, P4, P2tog (12sts)
  Right leg: P2tog, P4, P2tog, P5, P2tog (12sts)
- 5th row: K
- 6th row: P3, cast off 5, P3 (7sts)
- 7th row: K3, K2tog, K2 (6sts)
- Work 3 rows SS, starting with P
- 11th row: K1, inc in next, K2, inc in next, K1 (8sts)
- 12th row: P
- 13th row: K1, inc in next, K4, inc in next, K1 (10sts)
- 14th row: P
- 15th row: K1, inc in next, K6, inc in next, K1 (12sts)
- 16th row: P
- 17th row: K1, inc in next, K8, inc in next, K1 (14sts)

- Work 5 rows SS, starting with P
- 23th row: K1, sl1, K1, psso, K8, K2tog, K1 (12sts)
- 24th row: P1, P2tog, P6, P2tog, P1 (10sts)
- Work 4 rows SS, starting with K
- 29th row: K1, inc in next, K6, inc in next, K1 (12sts)
- Work 5 rows SS, starting with P
- 35th row: K1, inc in next, K8, inc in next, K1 (14sts)
- Work 5 rows SS, starting with P
- 41st row: K1, inc in next, K10, inc in next, K1 (16sts)
- 42nd row: P
- Cast off

To make up: Join seams. Stuff. Attach to body.

HEAD

COLOUR I
- Size 10/3.25mm needles

HEAD – FRONT (RIGHT SIDE)
- Cast on 5
- 1st row: K
- 2nd row: P
- 3rd row: Cast on 2, K to end (7sts)
- 4th row: P4, inc in next, inc in next, P1 (9sts)
- 5th row: K1, inc in next, K1, inc in next, K5 (11sts)
- 6th row: P11 – break wool, leave sts on needle

HEAD – FRONT (LEFT SIDE)
- With WS facing cast on 5, turn – now working on these 5sts only:
- 1st row: K

- 2nd row: P
- 3rd row: K, cast on 2 (7sts)
- 4th row: P1, inc in next, inc in next, P4 (9sts)
- 5th row: K5, inc in next, K1, inc in next, K1 (11sts)
- 6th row: P11
- To join 2 pieces together:
- 7th row: K7, inc in next, K2, K2tog, K2, inc in next, K7 (23sts)
- 8th row: P1, P2tog, P17, P2tog, P1 (21sts)
- Work 6 rows SS, starting with K
- 15th row: K2tog, K17, K2tog (19sts)
- 16th row: P
- 17th row: K2tog, K15, K2tog (17sts)
- 18th row: P4, P2tog, P5, P2tog, P4 (15sts)
- 19th row: K2tog, K2tog, K7, K2tog, K2tog (11sts)
- Cast off

HEAD – BACK
- Cast on 4
- 1st row: K
- 2nd row: P
- 3rd row: K
- 4th row: P row – inc in first and last st (6sts)
- 5th row: K row – inc in 1st and last (8sts)
- 6th row: P
- 7th row: K row – inc in 1st and last (10sts)
- Work 8 rows SS, starting with P
- 16th row: P1, P2tog, P6, P2tog, P1 (8sts)
- 17th row: K
- Cast off

To make up: Join seam under chin. Join front and back tog. Stuff. Attach to body

SKIRT

COLOUR 4
- Size 11/3.00mm needles

- Cast on 46
- Work 4 rows SS, starting with K
- 5th row: K14, inc in next, K19, inc in next, K11 (48sts)
- 6th row: P
- 7th row: Cast off 3, K to end (45sts)
- Work 3 rows SS, starting with P
- 11th row: K12, inc in next, K19, inc in next, K12 (47sts)
- Work 11 rows SS, starting with P
- 23th row: K12, K2tog, K19, K2tog, K12 (45sts)
- Work 3 rows SS, starting with P
- 27th row: K11, K2tog, K19, K2tog, K11 (43sts)
- 28th row: P
- 29th row: K9, K2tog, K1, K2tog, K15, K2tog, K1, K2tog, K9 (39sts)
- 30th row: P
- 31st row: K10, K2tog, K15, K2tog, K10 (37sts)
- Cast off

To make up: Press under damp cloth. Join centre seam at back, leaving the kick-pleat open.

CARDIGAN

COLOUR 3
- Size 12/2.75mm needles

- Cast on 45
- 1st row: K
- 2nd row: K2, P41, K2
- Repeat rows 1 and 2 once more

- Work 3 rows in K
- 8th row: K2, P41, K2
- 9th row: K
- Repeat rows (8 and 9) x 6
- 22nd row: K2, P41, K2
- 23rd row: K11, cast off 2, K18, cast off 2, K10
- Working on 11 sts for left front:
- 24th row: K2, P9
- 25th row: K2tog, K9 (10sts)
- 26th row: K2, P8
- 27th row: K
- 28th row: K3, P7
- 29th row: K
- 30th row: K3, P7
- 31st row: K
- 32nd row: K3, P5, P2tog (9sts)
- 33rd row: K
- 34th row: K4, P5
- 35th row: K
- 36th row: K4, P5
- 37th row: Cast off 3, K1, turn, put remaining 4 sts on pin for collar
- 38th row: Cast off 2
- With WS facing, now working on next 19 sts for the back
- 24th row: P
- 25th row: K2tog, K15, K2tog (17sts)
- Work 5 rows SS, starting with P
- 31st row: K2tog, K13, K2tog (15sts)
- 32nd row: P
- 33rd row: K5, turn –
- 34th row: P5
- 35th row: Cast off 5, K9 (10sts)
- 36th row: P5, turn –
- 37th row: K5
- Cast off

WITH WS FACING, NOW WORKING ON REMAINING 11 STS FOR THE RIGHT

FRONT

- 24th row: P9, K2
- 25th row: K9, K2tog (10sts)
- 26th row: P8, K2
- 27th row: K
- 28th row: P7, K3
- 29th row: K
- 30th row: P7, K3
- 31st row: K
- 32nd row: P2tog, P5, K3 (9sts)
- 33rd row: K
- 34th row: P5, K4
- 35th row: K
- 36th row: P5, K4
- 37th row: K
- 38th row: Cast off 5, K3 (4sts)
- These 4 sts are for the shawl collar, which is worked in GS
- Work 4 rows K
- 43rd row: K2, turn –
- 44th row: K2
- 45th row: K3, turn –
- 46th row: K3
- Work 4 rows K
- 51st row: K3, turn –
- 52nd row: K3
- Work 3 rows K
- Cast off
- With RS facing working on the 4 sts from left side front:
- Work 5 rows K
- 44th row: K2, turn –
- 45th row: K2
- 46th row: K3, turn –
- 47th row: K3
- Work 4 rows K
- 52nd row: K3, turn –
- 53rd row: K3

- Work 4 rows K
- Cast off

To make up: Press under damp cloth. Join shoulder seams. Join collar at centre back and sew around neckline.

SLEEVES – MAKE TWO
COLOUR 3

- Size 12/2.75mm needles

- Cast on 16
- Work 3 rows SS, starting with K
- Work 3 rows P
- Work 2 rows SS, starting with K
- 9th row: K row inc in 1st and last (18sts)
- Work 12 rows SS, starting with P
- 22nd row: Cast off 2, P to end (16sts)
- 23rd row: Cast off 2, K to end (14sts)
- 24th row: P2tog, P10, P2tog (12sts)
- 25th row: K
- 26th row: P9, turn –
- 27th row: K6, turn –
- 28th row: P5, P2tog, P2 (11sts)
- 29th row: K7, K2tog, K2 (10sts)
- 30th row: P2tog, P6, P2tog (8sts)
- 31st row: K
- 32nd row: P
- 33rd row: K3, K2tog, K3 (7sts)
- Cast off working first 2 and last 2 sts together

To make up: Press under damp cloth. Join seams. Inset in cardigan.
Dress doll. Add beads as buttons on jacket front.

JUMPER – FRONT ONLY
COLOUR 5

- Size 12/2.75mm needles

- Cast on 20
- Work 3 rows 1 and 1 rib
- 4th row: P
- 5th row: K1, inc in next, K16, inc in next, K1 (22sts)
- Work 3 rows SS, starting with P
- 9th row: K1, inc in next, K18, inc in next, K1 (24sts)
- 10th row: P
- 11th row: K1, inc in next, K20, inc in next, K1 (26sts)
- Work 4 rows SS, starting with P
- 16th row: P2tog, P22, P2tog (24sts)
- Work 3 rows SS, starting with K
- 20th row: Cast off 2, P to end (22sts)
- 21st row: Cast off 2, K to end (20sts)
- 22nd row: P
- 23rd row: K2tog, K16, K2tog (18sts)
- 24th row: P
- 25th row: K2tog, K14, K2tog (16sts)
- 26th row: P
- 27th row: K
- 28th row: P2tog, P4, turn –
- 29th row: K5
- 30th row: Cast off 10, P4
- 31st row: K5
- Cast off

Attach jumper front to doll, stitching at shoulders and sides

HANDBAG

COLOUR 6
- Size 12/2.75mm needles

- Cast on 14
- 1st row: K
- 2nd row: K
- 3rd row: K
- 4th row: K
- 5th row: Cast on 3 – P3, K14 (17sts)
- 6th row: Cast on 3 – K3, P14, K3 (20sts)
- 7th row: P3, K14, P3
- 8th row: K3, P14, K3
- 9th row: P3, K14, P3
- 10th row: K3, P14, K3
- 11th row: P3, K14, P3
- 12th row: K3, P14, K3
- 13th row: P3, K14, P3
- 14th row: K
- 15th row: P3, K14, P3
- 16th row: K3, P14, K3
- 17th row: P3, K14, P3
- 18th row: K3, P14, K3
- 19th row: P
- 20th row: K3, P14, K3
- 21st row: P3, K14, P3
- 22nd row: K3, P14, K3
- 23rd row: P3, K14, P3
- 24th row: K3, P14, K3
- 25th row: P3, K14, P3
- 26th row: K3, P14, K3
- 27th row: Cast off 3, K13, P3 (17sts)
- 28th row: Cast off 3, P13 (14sts)
- 29th row: K
- 30th row: K
- 31st row: K
- 32nd row: K
- Cast off

To make up: Fold in sides and iron under damp cloth. Working inside out, join side seams. Cut small piece of card and fit into bottom of bag to hold shape.

TO MAKE HANDLE
Using 3.00mm crochet hook, make a length of chain and attach to bag. Stitch on the two bronze coloured beads to make a bag fastener.

SHOES – MAKE TWO

COLOUR 3
- Size 12/ 2.75mm needles

- Cast on 3
- 1st row: K
- 2nd row: P3 cast on 11 (14sts)
- 3rd row: K9 turn –
- 4th row: P7 turn –
- 5th row: K12
- 6th row: P2tog, P12 (13sts)
- 7th row: K9 turn –
- 8th row: P6 turn –
- 9th row: K10
- 10th row: P5 turn –
- 11th row: K5
- 12th row: Cast off 8, P4
- 13th row: K4
- 14th row: P3 turn –
- 15th row: K4 cast on 8 (12sts)
- 16th row: P10 turn –
- 17th row: K10
- 18th row: P12 turn –
- 19th row: K5 turn –
- 20th row: P6
- 21st row: K12, inc in next (14sts)
- 22nd row: P14
- 23rd row: Cast off 11, K2 (3sts)
- 24th row: P3
- Cast off

To make up: Press flat under damp cloth. Close centre back heel seam. Close heel and seam on underside of shoe. Place on foot. A catching stitch will ensure it stays on.

HAIR

COLOUR 3

Daphne's hair is made out of small, uncut hanks of yarn; the loops help to give her hair a thick, slightly unkept, layered bob.

Cut a number of pieces of yarn approx. 52cm in length. Fold each length over twice to form small, uncut hanks. These hanks form the top layer of the hair. Fold each hank and using fine thread, attach to the hairline at the front and along crown parting. Place one hank at a time. Use small catching stitches to attach to head where necessary. For added shape and fullness, make a number of shorter hanks and attach at the back of the head in two horizontal lines underneath. Catch where necessary. Stitch in some shorter looped pieces to form a fringe. Use the embroidery thread to add some finishing loops in black to break up the flat brown colour (break down to 3 strands).

TO CREATE FACE

The nose is fashioned from a crocheted chain of flesh coloured wool – be generous. The ears are formed from a crocheted chain curled around on itself and stitched together. Add beads for eyes and yarn of your choice for brows and mouth. Daphne has a very expressive face. Refer to a cartoon to copy one of her many and varied expressions.

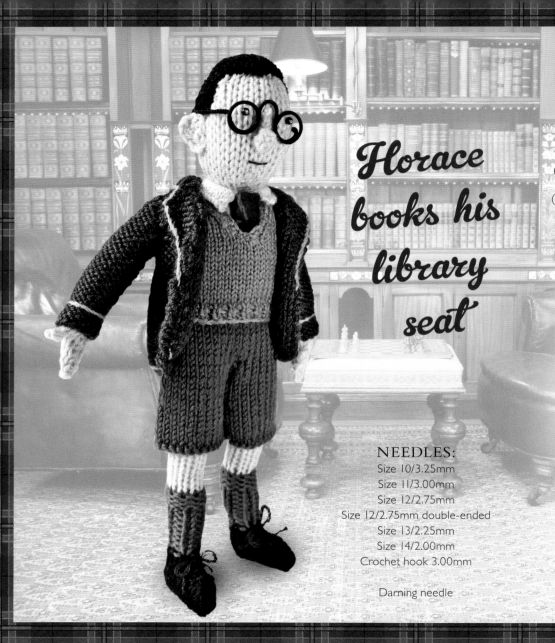

Horace books his library seat

You will need

MATERIALS:

Colour Codes:
1 Rowan Baby Merino Silk DK
(Shade SH674 – Shell Pink) – For Body
2 Debbie Bliss Baby Cashmerino
(Shade 340011 – Brown) – For Shoes and Hair
3 Debbie Bliss Baby Cashmerino
(Shade 340058 – Grey) – For Shorts and Socks
4 Debbie Bliss Baby Cashmerino
(Shade 340076 – Maroon) – For Tie
5 Debbie Bliss Rialto Lace
(Shade 44001 – Cream) – For Shirt
6 Debbie Bliss Rialto Lace (Use double)
(Shade 44003 – Grey) – For Slipover
7 Sublime Baby Cashmerino Silk DK
(Shade 0160 – Blue) – For Blazer
8 Sublime Baby Cashmerino Silk DK
(Shade 0383 – Yellow) – for Blazer Trim
9 Sublime Lace Extra Fine Merino Wool
(Shade 0398 – Charcoal) – For Hair
10 Rowan Fine Lace (Shade 00935 – Vamp) –
For Tie Stripe – small amount used
Alternative to 10 – Hank of red
embroidery thread

Beads for jacket buttons and eyes
Yarn for creating facial features
Small amount brown embroidery thread
Small amount of black millinery wire
Jewellery pliers
Stuffing

NEEDLES:
Size 10/3.25mm
Size 11/3.00mm
Size 12/2.75mm
Size 12/2.75mm double-ended
Size 13/2.25mm
Size 14/2.00mm
Crochet hook 3.00mm

Darning needle

Horace

Horace Broon is quite cheerful for someone who is constantly tormented by his younger brothers and has been in short trousers for over 75 years. He is the brains of the family. Before the Internet was invented, if the Broons needed information, they just asked Horace. His varied attempts to bring some culture to Glebe Street invariably end up in frustration.

Although the family often laugh at poetry Horace writes, he would tell them, on what he's trained his sights. "There I'd be, kent by all, my illustrious name side by side wi' Rabbie Burns, in Scotland's Hall of Fame."

BODY

COLOUR 1
- Size 10/3.25mm needles

BODY – FRONT
- Cast on 14
- 1st row: P
- 2nd row: K1, inc in next, K10, inc in next, K1 (16sts)
- Work 3 rows SS, starting with P
- 6th row: K1, (K2tog, K2) x3 K2tog, K1 (12sts)
- Work 3 rows SS, starting with P
- 10th row: K2, inc in next, K6, inc in next, K2 (14sts)
- 11th row: P
- 12th row: K2, inc in next, K8, inc in next, K2 (16sts)
- Work 6 rows SS, starting with P
- 19th row: P1, P2tog, P10, P2tog, P1 (14sts)
- 20th row: K1, sl1, K1, psso, K8, K2tog, K1 (12sts)
- 21st row: P1, P2tog, P6, P2tog, P1 (10sts)
- 22nd row: K
- Cast off

BODY – BACK
- Cast on 14
- 1st row: P
- 2nd row: K2, inc in next, K1, inc in next, K4, inc in next, K1, inc in next, K2 (18sts)
- 3rd row: P
- 4th row: K3, inc in next, K1, inc in next, K6, inc in next, K1, inc in next, K3 (22sts)
- Work 2 rows SS, starting with P
- 7th row: P1, P2tog, P16, P2tog, P1 (20sts)
- 8th row: K
- 9th row: P2, P2tog, P1, P2tog, P6, P2tog, P1, P2tog, P2 (16sts)
- 10th row: K
- 11th row: P2, P2tog, P1, P2tog, P2, P2tog, P1, P2tog, P2 (12sts)
- Work 4 rows SS, starting with K
- 16th row: K1, inc in next, K3, inc in next, inc in next, K3, inc in next, K1 (16sts)
- Work 6 rows SS beginning with P
- 23rd row: P1, P2tog, P10, P2tog, P1 (14sts)
- 24th row: K1, sl1, K1, psso, K8, K2tog, K1 (12sts)
- 25th row: P1, P2tog, P6, P2tog, P1 (10sts)
- 26th row: K
- Cast off

To make up: Join front to back. Stuff.

ARMS – MAKE TWO

COLOUR 1
- Size 10/3.25mm needles

WORKING FROM SHOULDER TO WRIST
- Cast on 4
- 1st row: K
- 2nd row: P
- 3rd row: K row – inc in 1st and last (6sts)
- 4th row: P
- 5th row: K row – inc in 1st and last (8sts)
- Work 21 rows starting with P

TO CREATE LEFT HAND
- 27th row: K2, put 2 on pin, K4
- 28th row: P to end bringing 2 sections together (6sts)
- 29th row: K
- 30th row: P1, P2tog, P2tog, P1 (4sts)
- 31st row: K2tog, K2tog (2sts)
- Pull thread through

TO CREATE RIGHT HAND
- 27th row: K4, put 2 on pin, K2
- 28th row: P to end bringing 2 sections together (6sts)
- 29th row: K
- 30th row: P1, P2tog, P2tog, P1 (4sts)
- 31st row: K2tog, K2tog (2sts)
- Pull thread through

THUMB – SAME FOR BOTH HANDS
- Size 12/2.75mm double-ended needles

- Put 2sts from pin on double-ended needle
- Join thread, K2
- K2tog as i-cord
- Pull thread through

To make up: Join seams. Stuff.

SHOES, SOCKS AND LEGS – MAKE TWO

COLOUR 2
- Size 10/3.25mm needles

- Cast on 18
- 1st row: K
- 2nd row: P7, P2tog, P2tog, P7 (16sts)
- 3rd row: K7, K2tog, K7 (15sts)
- 4th row: P
- 5th row: K4, cast off 6, K4 (9sts)
- 6th row: Pulling 2 sections together, P4, P2tog, P3 (8sts)
- Change to COLOUR 3 for Socks
- Work 4 rows 1 and 1 rib
- 11th row: Rib row, inc in 1st and last (10sts)
- Work 4 rows in rib
- Work 3 rows in SS, starting with K

- Change to COLOUR 1
- Work 2 rows SS, starting with K
- 21st row: K2tog, K6, K2tog (8sts)
- 22nd row: P
- 23rd row: K row, inc in 1st and last (10sts)
- Work 7 rows SS, starting with P
- 31st row: K row, inc in 1st and last (12sts)
- Work 8 rows SS, starting with P
- Cast off

To make up: Sew-up sole of shoe – stuff shoe. Join leg seam and stuff. Add shoelaces using the brown embroidery thread.

Tip: Stuff shoes with offcuts of brown wool rather than white wadding, which tends to show through.

HEAD

COLOUR 1
- Size 10/3.25mm needles

HEAD – BACK
- Cast on 5
- 1st row: K
- 2nd row: P
- 3rd row: K row, inc in 1st and last (7sts)
- 4th row: P
- 5th row: K row, inc in 1st and last (9sts)
- 6th row: P
- 7th row: K row, inc in 1st and last (11sts)
- 8th row: P
- 9th row: K2, (inc in next) x3, K1, (inc in next) x3, K2 (17sts)
- Work 5 rows starting with P
- 15th row: K1, sl1, K1, psso, K2, sl1, K1, psso, K3, K2tog, K2, K2tog, K1 (13sts)
- 16th row: P

- 17th row: (sl1, K1, psso)x3, K1, (K2tog)x3 (7sts)
- 18th row: P
- Cast off

HEAD – FRONT (RIGHT SIDE)
- Cast on 4
- 1st row: K
- 2nd row: P
- 3rd row: Cast on 2, K to end (6sts)
- 4th row: P5, inc in last (7sts)
- 5th row: Inc in 1st, inc in next, K5 (9sts)
- 6th row: P9 – break wool, leave sts on needle

HEAD – FRONT (LEFT SIDE)
- With WS facing cast on 4, turn – now working on these 4sts only:
- 1st row: K
- 2nd row: P
- 3rd row: K to end, cast on 2 (6sts)
- 4th row: Inc in 1st, P5 (7sts)
- 5th row: K5, inc in next, inc in next (9sts)
- 6th row: P9
- 7th row: Work across 2 pieces to join, K8, K2tog, K8 (17sts)
- Work 4 rows SS, starting with P
- 12th row: P2tog, P13, P2tog (15sts)
- 13th row: K
- 14th row: P2tog, P11, P2tog (13sts)
- 15th row: K
- 16th row: P2tog, P9, P2tog (11sts)
- 17th row: K2tog, K7, K2tog (9sts)
- 18th row: P
- Cast off

To make up: Join seam under chin. Join front and back tog. Stuff. Attach to body.

SHIRT

SHIRT FRONT
COLOUR 5
- Size 13/2.25mm needles

- Cast on 20
- Work 22 rows SS, starting with K
- 23rd row: K7, turn –
- 24th row: P7
- 25th row: K
- 26th row: P7
- 27th row: K7
- Cast off

To make up: Stitch onto body front at shoulders and hips.

COLLAR

COLOUR 5
- Size 14/2.00mm needles

- Cast on 28
- 1st row: K
- 2nd row: K1, P26, K1
- 3rd row: K
- 4th row: K1, P26, K1
- 5th row: K1, inc in next, K5, inc in next, K1, inc in next, K8, inc in next, K1, inc in next, K5, inc in next, K1 (34sts)
- 6th row: K1, P32, K1
- 7th row: K
- 8th row: K1, P32, K1
- 9th row: K row, inc in last
- Cast off

To make up: Fold and iron under a damp cloth. Attach around neck and to shirt front.

SHORTS

COLOUR 3

- Size 12/2.75mm needles

RIGHT LEG

- Cast on 25
- Work 12 rows SS, starting with K
- 13th row: K1, inc in next, K21, inc in next, K1 (27sts)
- 14th row: P
- 15th row: Cast off 2, K to end (25sts)
- 16th row: Cast off 2, P to end (23sts)
- 17th row: K
- 18th row: P
- Hold on pin

LEFT LEG

- Cast on 25
- Work as right leg to row 18

KNITTING LEGS TOGETHER, STARTING WITH LEFT LEG

- 19th row: K2tog, K20, K last stitch of left leg with first stitch of right leg – K20, K2tog (43sts)
- Work 4 rows SS, starting with P
- 29th row: P11, P2tog, P17, P2tog, P11, (41sts)
- 30th row: K
- 31st row: P5, P2tog, P4, P2tog, P15, P2tog, P4, P2tog, P5 (37sts)
- 32nd row: (K4, K2tog) x2, K13, (K2tog, K4) x2 (33sts)
- Cast off

To make up: Join inside leg seams. Join crotch. Dress doll.

SLIPOVER – (FRONT ONLY)

COLOUR 6 – USE DOUBLED

- Size 12/2.75mm needles

- Cast on 28
- Work 3 rows in 1 and 1 rib
- Work 13 rows SS, starting with K
- 17th row: Cast off 3, P9, cast off 2, P12
- 18th row: Cast off 3, K9, turn –
- Now working on left front
- 19th row: K1, P6, P2tog, K1 (9sts)
- 20th row: K
- 21st row: K1, P2tog, P5, K1 (8sts)
- 22nd row: K
- 23rd row: K1, P6, K1
- 24th row: K5, K2tog, K1 (7sts)
- 25th row: K1, P5, K1
- 26th row: K4, K2tog, K1 (6sts)
- 27th row: K1, P4, K1
- 28th row: K
- Cast off

NOW WORKING ON RIGHT FRONT – WITH RS FACING JOIN WOOL AT CENTRE FRONT NECK

- 18th row: K10
- 19th row: K1, P2tog, P6, K1 (9sts)
- 20th row: K
- 21st row: K1, P5, P2tog, K1 (8sts)
- 22nd row: K
- 23rd row: K1, P6, K1
- 24th row: K1, sl1, K1, psso, K5 (7sts)
- 25th row: K1, P5, K1
- 26th row: K1, sl1, K1, psso, K4 (6sts)
- 27th row: K1, P4, K1
- 28th row: K
- Cast off

To make up: Finish and tidy V-neck edge with reverse single crochet edging. Join to front of doll.

BLAZER

COLOUR 7

- Size 11/3.00mm needles

MAIN BODY – THIS IS WORKED IN REVERSE SS

- Cast on 40
- 1st row: K
- 2nd row: K1, P38, K1
- 3rd row: K1, inc in next, K36, inc in next, K1 (42sts)
- 4th row: K1, P40, K1
- 5th row: K1, inc in next, K38, inc in next, K1 (44sts)
- 6th row: K1, P42, K1
- 7th row: K
- 8th row: As row 6
- 9th row: K
- 10th row: As row 6
- 11th row: K
- 12th row: As row 6
- 13th row: K
- 14th row: As row 6
- 15th row: K
- 16th row: As row 6
- 17th row: K
- 18th row: K1, inc in next, P40, inc in next, K1 (46sts)
- 19th row: K1, P1, K42, P1, K1
- 20th row: K2, P42, K2
- 21st row: K1, P2, K9, cast off 2, K17, cast off 2, K8, P2, K1
- Working on right front (12sts)
- 22nd row: K3, P9

- 23rd row: K2tog, K7, P2, K1 (11sts)
- 24th row: K4, P7
- 25th row: K7, P3, K1
- 26th row: K4, P7
- 27th row: K2tog, K4, P4, K1 (10sts)
- 28th row: K5, P5
- 29th row: K5, P4, K1
- 30th row: Cast off 3, K1, P5 (7sts)
- 31st row: K5, put last 2 sts on pin for collar, turn –
- 32nd row: P5
- 33rd row: K5
- Cast off

WORKING ON JACKET BACK – NEXT 18 STS – RS FACING (REVERSE SS)

- Work 3 rows SS, starting with P
- 25th row: K2tog, K14, K2tog (16sts)
- 26th row: P
- 27th row: K
- 28th row: P2tog, P12, P2tog (14sts)
- Work 3 rows starting with K
- 32nd row: Cast off 4, P9 (10sts)
- 33rd row: Cast off 4, leave 6 sts on pin for collar

WORKING ON LEFT FRONT (REMAINING 12STS)

- 22nd row: P9, K3
- 23rd row: K1, P2, K7, K2tog (11sts)
- 24th row: P7, K4
- 25th row: K1, P3, K7
- 26th row: P7, K4
- 27th row: K1, P4, K4, K2tog (10sts)
- 28th row: P5, K5
- 29th row: K1, P4, K5
- 30th row: P5, K5
- 31st row: Cast off 3, P1, K5 (7sts)

- 32nd row: P5, put last 2 sts on pin for collar, turn –
- 33rd row: K5
- Cast off

To make up: Join shoulder seams.

UPPER COLLAR
- Size 12/2.75mm needles

WORKING WITH RS FACING (RIGHT SIDE IS REVERSE SS)
- 1st row: K2 sts from right lapel, pick up 5 sts along right front neck, K6 from back neck, pick up 5 sts along left front neck, K2 sts from left lapel (20sts)
- 2nd row: K1, P18, K1
- 3rd row: K6, inc in next, K6, inc in next, K6 (22sts)
- 4th row: K1, P20, K1
- Cast off loosely

To make up: Steam press to tidy collar and lapels.

BLAZER SLEEVES – MAKE TWO
- Size 11/3.00mm needles

- Cast on 13
- Work 12 rows SS, starting with K
- 13th row: For left sleeve, K9, inc in next, K3 (14sts) For right sleeve, K3, inc in next, K9 (14sts)
- Work 6 rows SS, starting with P
- 20th row: Cast off 1, P to end (13sts)
- 21st row: Cast off 1, K to end (12sts)
- 22nd row: P2tog, P8, P2tog (10sts)

- 23rd row: K
- 24th row: P2tog, P6, P2tog (8sts)
- 25th row: K3, K2tog, K3 (7sts)
- 26th row: P
- Cast off

To make up: Join seams. Inset to jacket. Using 3 strands of COLOUR 8 work a trim around the edge of the blazer and blazer cuffs (stem stitch used). Add beads for buttons. Dress doll.

TIE

COLOUR 4
- Size 12/2.75mm needles

- Cast on 6
- Work 4 rows SS, starting with K
- 5th row: K1, K2tog, K2tog, K1 (4sts)
- 6th row: P
- Work 20 rows SS, starting with K
- 27th row: K1, K2tog, K1 (3sts)
- Continue in SS for 13 rows starting with P
- Cast off

To make up: Steam press flat. Fold into a point at wide end and stitch in place. Add diagonal stripes in stem stitch using COLOUR 10. Fold in half. Make a knot and stitch in place around neck.

HAIR

COLOUR 2
- Size 3.25mm needles

Tip: Make and attach ears and nose before hairpiece. See TO CREATE FACE.

- Cast on 12
- Work 4 rows SS, starting with K
- 5th row: K1, inc in next, K8, K1 (14sts)
- Work 3 rows SS, starting with P
- 9th row: Cast on 2, K16 (16sts)
- 10th row: Cast on 2, P18 (18sts)
- 11th row: K5, K2tog, K4, K2tog, K5 (16sts)
- 12th row: P
- 13th row: K2tog, K12, K2tog (14sts)
- 14th row: P2tog, P10, P2tog (12sts)
- 15th row: K2, K2tog, K4, K2tog, K2 (10sts)
- 16th row: P8, turn –
- 17th row: K6, turn –
- 18th row: P8 (10sts)
- 19th row: K9, turn –
- 20th row: P8, turn –
- 21st row: K9 (10sts)
- 22nd row: P2tog, P6, P2tog, (8sts)
- 23rd row: K2tog, K4, K2tog (6sts)
- 24th row: P2tog, P2, P2tog (4sts)
- 25th row: K4
- 26th row: P2tog, P2tog (2sts)
- Cast off

To make up: Pin in place and stitch. Cut lengths of COLOUR 9. Thread a darning needle and overlay long stitches from front hairline to back of crown to suggest comb-back.

TO CREATE FACE

Referring to a chosen cartoon will help capture our high-minded Horace.

Add beads for eyes. The nose and ears are fashioned from crocheted chains of the flesh-coloured wool. Pin and stitch on when you feel you have a good likeness. Add eyebrows and mouth.

SPECTACLES

Grip a cut piece of the wire (approx. 20cm) with the jewellery pliers and wind round a fat knitting needle or pencil to shape lenses. Fold back legs at right angles and trim to desired length, folding in any sharp ends. Add to face and secure with one or two stitches.

The outlaw Twins!

You will need

MATERIALS:

Colour Codes:
1 Rowan Baby Merino Silk DK
(Shade SH674 – Shell Pink) – For Body
2 Hayfield Bonus DK
(Shade 0947 – Brown) – For Sandals
3 Rowan Baby Cashmerino Silk DK
(Shade Deep 682 – Blue) – For Shorts
4 Rowan Wool Cotton
(Shade 00911 – Red) – For Jumper
5 Regia Angora Merino
(Shade 07081 – Pale Grey) – For Socks
6 Sublime Baby Cashmerino Silk DK
(Shade 0383 – Yellow) – For Hair –
pare down to single strands
7 Hank of tapestry wool – golden yellow –
For Hair

Beads for buttons on jumper, sandals and eyes
Yarn for creating facial features
Stuffing

NEEDLES:

Size 10/3.25mm
Size 9/3.75mm
Size 12/2.75mm
Size 12/2.75mm double-ended
Crochet hook 3.00mm
Crochet hook 1.5mm
Darning needle

The Twins

Wi' the Twins, first and last,
some-thing good tae eat,
jellies, ice-cream, chocolate
anything that's sweet.
Munchin', gobblin', stappit moo's,
nae thocht of' tummy-ache.
Whit they say is true enough,
"OOR wish tak's the cake!"

Perhaps we can put the sometimes unruly behaviour of the Broons Twins down to them being deficient of first names - they are only ever called The Twins, or sometimes Ae Twin and Ither Twin. Fond of fighting, catties, bogies, fitba in the street, sliding and scrumping aipples. They don't like lassies, bath night, housework, school or sharing.

BODY

COLOUR 1
- Size 10/3.25mm needles

BODY – FRONT
- Cast on 12
- 1st row: K
- 2nd row: P row, inc in 1st and last (14sts)
- 3rd row: K
- 4th row: (P1, P2tog) x2, P2, (P2tog, P1) x2 (10sts)
- Work 2 rows SS, starting with K
- 7th row: K2, inc in next, K4, inc in next, K2 (12sts)
- 8th row: P
- 9th row: K2, inc in next, K6, inc in next, K2 (14sts)
- Work 5 rows SS, starting with P
- 15th row: K2tog, K10, K2tog (12sts)
- 16th row: P
- 17th row: K1, sl1, K1, psso, K6, K2tog, K1 (10sts)
- 18th row: P1, P2tog, P4, P2tog, P1 (8sts)
- 19th row: K
- Cast off

BODY – BACK
- Cast on 12
- 1st row: P
- 2nd row: K1, inc in next, K1, inc in next, K4, inc in next, K1, inc in next, K1 (16sts)
- 3rd row: P
- 4th row: K3, inc in next, K8, inc in next, K3 (18sts)
- Work 2 rows SS, starting with P
- 7th row: (P1, P2tog) x2, P6, (P2tog, P1) x2 (14sts)
- 8th row: K

- 9th row: (P1, P2tog) x2, P2, (P2tog, P1) x2 (10sts)
- Work 2 rows starting with K
- 12th row: K2, inc in next, K1, inc in next, inc in next, K1, inc in next, K2 (14sts)
- Work 6 rows SS, starting with K
- 16th row: K1, inc in next, K3, inc in next, inc in next, K3, inc in next, K1 (16sts)
- Work 6 rows SS beginning with P
- 19th row: P1, P2tog, P8, P2tog, P1 (12sts)
- 20th row: K1, sl1, K1, psso, K6, K2tog, K1 (10sts)
- 21st row: P1, P2tog, P4, P2tog, P1 (8sts)
- 22nd row: K
- Cast off

To make up: Join front to back. Stuff.

ARMS – MAKE TWO

COLOUR 1
- Size 10/3.25mm needles

WORKING FROM SHOULDER TO WRIST
- Cast on 3
- 1st row: K
- 2nd row: P row inc in 1st and last (5sts)
- 3rd row: K
- 4th row: P row inc in 1st and last (7sts)
- Work 19 rows SS, starting with K
- 24th row: P3, P2tog, P2 (6sts)

TO CREATE LEFT HAND
- 25th row: K1, put 2 on pin, K3 (4sts)
- 26th row: P to end bringing 2 sections together (4sts)
- 27th row: K
- 28th row: P2tog, P2tog, (2sts)
- Pull thread through

TO CREATE RIGHT HAND
- 25th row: K3, put 2 on pin, K1 (4sts)
- 26th row: P to end bringing 2 sections together (4sts)
- 27th row: K
- 28th row: P2tog, P2tog, (2sts)
- Pull thread through

THUMB – SAME FOR BOTH HANDS

- Size 12/2.75mm double-ended needles

- Put 2sts from pin on double-ended needle
- Join thread, K2
- K2tog as i-cord
- Pull thread through

To make up: Join seams. Stuff.

SHOES, SOCKS AND LEGS – MAKE TWO

COLOUR 2

- Size 10/3.25mm needles

- Cast on 14
- 1st row: K
- 2nd row: P5, P2tog, P2tog, P5 (12sts)
- 3rd row: K5, K2tog, K5 (11sts)
- 4th row: P
- Change to COLOUR 5 for Sock
- 5th row: K
- 6th row: P3, cast off 4, P3 (7sts)
- 7th row: K3, K2tog, K2 (6sts)
- Work 3 rows SS, starting with P
- 11th row: P
- Change to COLOUR 1
- Work 3 rows in SS, starting with P
- 15th row: K row – inc 1st and last (8sts)
- Work 2 rows SS, starting P
- 18th row: P2tog, P4, P2tog (6sts)
- 19th row: K
- 20th row: P row inc 1st and last (8sts)
- Work 6 rows SS, starting with K
- 27th row: K row, inc 1st and last (10sts)
- Work 6 rows SS, starting with P
- Cast off

To make up: Sew-up sole of shoe – stuff shoe. Join leg seam and stuff. To finish sandals make a T-bar out of a crocheted chain of COLOUR 2. Stitch to shoe and add a bead as a buckle fastening.

Tip: Stuff shoes with offcuts of brown wool rather than white wadding, which tends to show through.

HEAD

COLOUR 1

- Size 10/3.25mm needles

HEAD – BACK

- Cast on 4
- 1st row: K
- 2nd row: P
- 3rd row: K row, inc in 1st and last (6sts)
- 4th row: P
- 5th row: K1, (inc in next) x4, K1 (10sts)
- 6th row: P
- 7th row: K row, inc in 1st and last (12sts)
- Work 6 rows starting with P
- 14th row: P2tog, P8, P2tog (10sts)
- 15th row: K
- 16th row: P1, (P2tog) x4, P1 (6sts)
- 17th row: K
- Cast off

HEAD – FRONT (RIGHT SIDE)

- Cast on 4
- 1st row: P
- 2nd row: K
- 3rd row: P to end, cast on 2 (6sts)
- 4th row: Inc in 1st, inc in next, K4 (8sts)
- 5th row: P
- Break wool, leave sts on needle

HEAD – FRONT (LEFT SIDE)

- With WS facing cast on 4, turn – now working on these 4sts only:
- 1st row: P
- 2nd row: K
- 3rd row: Cast on 2, P to end (6sts)
- 4th row: K4, inc in next, inc in last (8sts)
- 5th row: P
- 6th row: Work across 2 pieces to join, K7, K2tog, K7 (15sts)
- Work 8 rows SS, starting with P
- 15th row: P2tog, P11, P2tog (13sts)
- 16th row: K2tog, K9, K2tog (11sts)
- 17th row: P2tog, P7, P2tog (9sts)
- 18th row: K2tog, K5, K2tog (7sts)
- Cast off

To make up: Join seam under chin. Join front and back tog. Stuff. Attach to body.

JUMPER – FRONT

COLOUR 4

- Size 12/2.75mm double-ended needles

- Cast on 28 join into a circle
- Work 16 rounds in K
- 17th row: Cast off 2, K11, turn – (12sts) (work on these sts as front)
- 18th row: P
- 19th row: K2tog, K8, K2tog (10sts)
- 20th row: P4, turn –
- 21st row: K2tog, K2
- 22nd row: P3, cast off 2, P3 (7sts)
- 23rd row: K2, K2tog, turn –
- 24th row: P3,
- 25th row: Cast off 3
- Now cast off 3 sts from right front shoulder
- With RS facing work on remaining 14 sts

- 17th row: Cast off 2, K11 (12sts)
- Work 3 rows SS, starting with P
- 21st row: K2tog, K8, K2tog (10sts)
- Work 3 rows SS, starting with P
- 25th row: Cast off 3, K3, cast off 3, leave remaining 4 sts on pin

JUMPER COLLAR
- Size 12/2.75mm needles

- Cast on 8 sts, with RS facing K4 sts from pin at back neck, cast on 9 sts (22sts)
- 1st row: K
- 2nd row: K1, P20, K1
- 3rd row: K
- 4th row: K1, inc in next, P18, inc in next, K1 (24sts)
- 5th row: K, inc in last st (25sts)
- Cast off

SLEEVES – MAKE TWO

- Size 12/2.75mm needles

- Cast on 10 sts
- Work 12 rows starting with K
- 13th row: K row, for left sleeve inc in 1st, for right sleeve inc in last (11sts)
- Work 7 rows SS, starting with P
- 21st row: Cast off 1, K to end (10sts)
- 22nd row: Cast off 1, P to end (9sts)
- 23rd row: K2tog, K5, K2tog (7sts)
- 24th row: P2tog, P3, P2tog (5sts)
- Cast off

To make up: Join shoulder seam and collar on that side. Join sleeve seams and inset one sleeve. Put body of jumper on doll and sew up second shoulder seam. Join collar. Inset second sleeve on doll. Add 3 small red beads for buttons.

SHORTS

COLOUR 3
- Size 12/2.75mm needles

RIGHT LEG
- Cast on 22
- 1st row: P
- 2nd row: P
- Work 6 rows SS, starting with K
- 9th row: K1, inc in next, K18, inc in next, K1 (24sts)
- 10th row: P
- 11th row: Cast off 2, K to end (22sts)
- 12th row: Cast off 2, P to end (20sts)
- Put aside

LEFT LEG
- Cast on 22
- Work as right leg to row 12

TO JOIN LEGS TOGETHER
- 13th row: K2tog, K17, K2tog (last from left leg and first from right leg), K17, K2tog (37sts)
- 14th row: P
- 15th row: K
- 16th row: P2tog, P33, P2tog (35sts)
- 17th row: K
- 18th row: P10, P2tog, P11, P2tog, P10 (33sts)
- 19th row: K9, K2tog, K11, K2tog, K9 (31sts)
- 20th row: P8, P2tog, P11, P2tog, P8 (29sts)
- 21st row: K
- Cast off

To make up: Join inside leg seams. Join crotch. Dress doll

HAIR

COLOUR 7
- Size 9/3.75 needles

Tip: It is easier to work on hair after ears and nose have been attached. See TO CREATE FACE.

- Cast on 8
- 1st row: K
- 2nd row: P
- 3rd row: K1, inc in next, K4, inc in next, K1 (10sts)
- 4th row: P
- 5th row: K1, inc in next, K6, inc in next, K1 (12sts)
- Work 3 rows SS, starting with P
- 9th row: K1, inc in next, K8, inc in next, K1 (14sts)
- 10th row: P
- 11th row: K1, inc in next, K10, inc in next, K1 (16sts)
- 12th row: P12 turn –
- 13th row: K8 turn –
- 14th row: P2tog, P4, P2tog, P4 (14sts)
- 15th row: K4, K2tog, K2, K2tog, K4 (12sts)
- 16th row: P9 turn –
- 17th row: K6 turn –
- 18th row: P9 (12sts)
- 19th row: Cast off 3, K8 (9sts)
- 20th row: Cast off 3, P5 (6sts)
- 21st row: K2tog, K2, K2tog (4sts)
- Cast off

To make up: Sew hairpiece to head – this acts as a base colour for the short hair. Cut workable lengths of COLOUR 7 and single strands of COLOUR 6. Steam press.

Working with no more than 2 or 3 pieces of yarn at a time, mix in and knot into the head using the smaller crochet hook or a darning needle. Work in yarns as closely as possible. Pay particular attention to the front hairline knotting in a few single strands of COLOUR 6 to finish. Trim short with hairdressing scissors.

Tip: Make over-long and trim when the whole head is covered.

TO CREATE FACE

Add beads for eyes. We used blue glass beads and tiny black beads for the pupil. The nose and ears are fashioned from crocheted chains of the flesh-coloured wool. Pin and stitch on when you feel you have a good likeness. Add eyebrows and mouth. Refer to a cartoon to capture the lively nature of the twins.

The Bairn's fun and games

You will need

MATERIALS:

Colour Codes:

1 Milla Mia Sweden Naturally soft Merino
(Shade Petal 122) – For Body and Dolly's body

2 Rowan Fine Tweed (Shade Skipton 379 –
Blue) – For Shoes and Dolly's shoes

3 Rowan Creative Linen
(Shade 640 – Sunflower) – For Frock

4 Rowan Fine Lace (Shade 00928 – Cream) –
For Frock Trim and Socks and Dolly's frock trim

5 Debbie Bliss Rialto Lace
(Shade 44002 – Pale Grey) – For Pants

6 Debbie Bliss Blue Faced Leicester DK
(Shade Ecru 46501 – Cream) – For Hair

7 Rowan Fine Lace
(Shade 00930 – Straw) – for Dolly's frock

Beads for eyes and Dolly's eyes
Yarn for creating facial features
Reel of cream sewing thread
Stuffing

NEEDLES:

Size 10/3.25mm

Size 10/3.25mm double-ended

Size 11/3.00mm

Size 12/2.75mm

Size 12/2.75mm double-ended

Size 13/2.25mm

Size 14/2.00mm

Size 9/3.75mm

Crochet hook 1.5mm

Crochet hook 3mm

Crochet hook 2.25mm

Darning needle

The Bairn

The youngest Broon, The Bairn, often manages to appear to be the most mature member of the family. Like a mini version of Maw, she likes to tell-off her siblings, and sometimes her parents, for bad behaviour. She loves her dollies and her Paw. She and Granpaw are best pals and she prefers to spend time with him than bairns her own age. Her misinterpretation of what she overhears from the adults is often the cause of the family's trademark mix-ups.

SUPPLEMENT TO THE SUNDAY POST,
SEPTEMBER 11, 1938.

Baby o' the family,
the Bairn's content tae be.
What she'd wish is something
all her chums could see.
China dolls wi' rosy cheeks,
an' bonnie golden hair.
And a braw new shiny pram,
tae tak' them oot for air.

BODY

COLOUR 1
- Size 10/3.25mm needles

BODY – FRONT
- Cast on 8
- 1st row: K
- 2nd row: P
- 3rd row: Inc in 1st, K1, inc in next, K2, inc in next, K1, inc in last (12sts)
- 4th row: P
- 5th row: Inc in 1st, K2, inc in next, K4, inc in next, K2, inc in last (16sts)
- Work 9 rows SS, starting with P
- 15th row: K3, K2tog, K6, K2tog, K3 (14sts)
- 16th row: P
- 17th row: K4, K2tog, K2, K2tog, K4 (12sts)
- 18th row: P
- 19th row: K
- 20th row: P2tog, P8, P2tog (10sts)
- 21st row: K2tog, K6, K2tog (8sts)
- Cast off

BODY – BACK
- Cast on 10
- 1st row: K
- 2nd row: P
- 3rd row: K row, inc in 1st and last (12sts)
- Work 14 rows SS, starting with P
- 18th row: P2tog, P8, P2tog (10sts)
- 19th row: K2tog, K6, K2tog (8sts)
- 20th row: P
- Cast off

To make up: Join front and back together. Stuff.

ARMS – MAKE TWO

COLOUR 1
- Size 10/3.25mm needles

WORKING FROM SHOULDER TO WRIST
- Cast on 3
- 1st row: K
- 2nd row: P
- 3rd row: K row inc in 1st and last (5sts)
- 4th row: P
- 5th row: K2, inc in next, K2 (6sts)
- Work 17 rows SS, starting with P

TO CREATE LEFT HAND
- 23rd row: K1, put 2 on pin, K3 (4sts)
- 24th row: P to end bringing 2 sections together (4sts)
- 25th row: K2tog, K2tog (2sts)
- Pull thread through

TO CREATE RIGHT HAND
- 23rd row: K3, put 2 on pin, K1 (4sts)
- 24th row: P to end bringing 2 sections together (4sts)
- 25th row: K2tog, K2tog (2sts)
- Pull thread through

THUMB – SAME FOR BOTH HANDS
- Size 12/2.75mm double-ended needles
- Put 2sts from pin on double-ended needle
- Join thread, K2
- K2tog as i-cord
- Pull thread through

To make up: Join seams. Stuff.

SOCKS AND LEGS – MAKE TWO

COLOUR 4 – use doubled
- Size 10/3.25mm needles
- Cast on 12
- 1st row: K
- 2nd row: P4, P2tog, P2tog, P4 (10sts)
- 3rd row: K4, K2tog, K4 (9sts)
- 4th row: P
- 5th row: K3, cast off 2, K3 (7sts)
- 6th row: P3, P2tog, P2 (6sts)
- 7th row: K
- 8th row: P
- 9th row: P
- 10th row: P row changing to COLOUR 1
- Work 8 rows SS, starting with K
- 19th row: K row inc in 1st and last (8sts)
- Work 7 rows SS, starting with P
- Cast off

To make up: Sew-up sole of sock – stuff sock. Join leg seam and stuff.

HEAD

COLOUR 1
- Size 10/3.25mm needles

HEAD – BACK
- Cast on 4
- 1st row: K
- 2nd row: P
- 3rd row: K row, inc in 1st and last (6sts)
- 4th row: P
- 5th row: K1, (inc in next) x4, K1 (10sts)
- 6th row: P
- 7th row: K row, inc in 1st and last (12sts)
- Work 6 rows starting with P
- 14th row: P2tog, P8, P2tog (10sts)
- 15th row: K
- 16th row: P1, (P2tog) x4, P1 (6sts)

- 17th row: K
- Cast off

HEAD – FRONT (RIGHT SIDE)
- Cast on 4
- 1st row: P
- 2nd row: K
- 3rd row: P to end, cast on 2 (6sts)
- 4th row: Inc in 1st, inc in next, K4 (8sts)
- 5th row: P
- Break wool, leave sts on needle

HEAD – FRONT (LEFT SIDE)
- With WS facing cast on 4, turn – now working on these 4sts only:
- 1st row: P
- 2nd row: K
- 3rd row: Cast on 2, P to end (6sts)
- 4th row: K4, inc in next, inc in last (8sts)
- 5th row: P
- 6th row: Work across 2 pieces to join, K7, K2tog, K7 (15sts)
- Work 8 rows SS, starting with P
- 15th row: P2tog, P11, P2tog (13sts)
- 16th row: K2tog, K9, K2tog (11sts)
- 17th row: P2tog, P7, P2tog (9sts)
- 18th row: K2tog, K5, K2tog (7sts)
- Cast off

To make up: Join seam under chin. Join front and back tog. Stuff. Attach to body.

DRESS

COLOUR 3
- Size 10/3.25mm double-ended needles

- Cast on 40 and join into a circle
- Work 8 rounds in K

- 9th row: K19, K2tog, K18, K last st tog with 1st st of next row (38sts)
- Work 5 rounds
- Working on 2 needles, next 19sts only (put other sts on pin)
- 15th row: (K2tog)x4, K3, (K2tog)x4 (11sts)
- Work 4 rows SS
- Cast off
- Working on back with right side facing
- 15th row: (K2tog)x4, K3, (K2tog)x4 (11sts)
- Work 4 rows SS
- Cast off

SLEEVES – MAKE TWO
- Cast on 10
- 1st row: P
- 2nd row: K4, inc in next, inc in next, K4 (12sts)
- 3rd row: P
- 4th row: K
- 5th row: P2tog, P8, P2tog (10sts)
- 6th row: K2tog, K6, K2tog (8sts)
- 7th row: P2tog, P4, P2tog (6sts)
- 8th row: K2tog, K2, K2tog (4sts)
- 9th row: P2tog, P2tog (2sts)
- Cast off

To make up: Press dress under a damp cloth. Dress doll and close shoulder seams. Close sleeve seams and inset.

DRESS COLLAR

COLOUR 4
- Size 14/2mm needles

The dress collar and hem frill are decorative frilled edgings stitched on. The repeat pattern is worked in groups of multiples of 7 sts plus 2 additional sts.

COLLAR
- Cast on 72
- 1st row: Wrong side *K2, P5; repeat from *, K2
- 2nd row: *P2, K1, sl 2tog knitwise, K1, p2sso, K1; repeat from *, P2
- 3rd row: *K2, P3; repeat from * K2
- 4th row: *P2, sl 2tog knitwise, K1, p2sso; repeat from * P2
- 5th row: *K2, P1; repeat from * K2
- 6th row: K
- Cast off

Stitch round neck of dress

DRESS FRILL
- Cast on 142
- Repeat collar pattern rows 1-6
- Cast off

Stitch round hem of dress

PANTS

COLOUR 5
- Size 14/2.00mm needles

STARTING ON BACK
- Cast on 22
- Work 13 rows SS, starting with K
- 14th row: P2tog, P18, P2tog (20sts)
- 15th row: Cast off 3, K16 (17sts)
- 16th row: Cast off 3, P13 (14sts)
- 17th row: K2tog, K10, K2tog (12sts)
- 18th row: P2tog, P8, P2tog (10sts)
- 19th row: K2tog, K6, K2tog (8sts)
- 20th row: P2tog, P4, P2tog (6sts)
- 21st row: K
- 22nd row: P

- 23rd row: Inc in first, K4, inc in last
- 24th row: Inc in first, P6, inc in last (10sts)
- 25th row: Inc in first, K8, inc in last (12sts)
- 26th row: Cast on 4, P16 (16sts)
- 27th row: Cast on 4, K20 (20sts)
- 28th row: Inc in first, P18, inc in last (22sts)
- Continue in SS for 13 rows starting with K
- Cast off

To make up: Press. Join side seams and add to doll.

SHOES
COLOUR 2
- Size 12/2.75 needles

STARTING AT BACK OF SHOE – LEFT SHOE
- Cast on 9
- 1st row: K
- Work 7 rows SS, starting with P
- 9th row: Cast off 2, K6 (7sts)
- 10th row: Cast off 2, P4, (5sts)
- 11th row: K
- 12th row: P
- 13th row: K2tog, K1, K2tog (3sts)
- 14th row: P
- 15th row: K
- Cast off

RIGHT SHOE
- As left but substitute the following 3 rows
- 8th row: Cast off 2, P6 (7sts)
- 9th row: Cast off 2, K4 (5sts)
- 10th row: P
- Continue as pattern for left shoe
- Cast off

To make up: Close heel seam and the two seams that form the closed front of shoe. Add to doll. With size 2.25 crochet hook make a chain shoe strap. Stitch on a bead for a button fastening.

HAIR
COLOUR 6
- Size 3.75 needle

Knit up a rectangle in SS approx 10cm x 4cm. Steam press and allow to dry. Unpick stitches to create crinkly wool. Cut into useable lengths and using a crochet hook or a darning needle, hook and tie in to head, catching close to the head with fine thread where necessary. Work from front to back of head and in small areas at a time to build texture.

TO CREATE FACE
Add beads for eyes. The nose and ears are fashioned from crocheted chains of the flesh-coloured wool- use 3mm crochet hook. Pin and stitch on when you feel you have a good likeness. Add eyebrows and mouth

Dolly

The Bairn's Dolly is a miniature version of herself!

BODY AND HEAD

COLOUR 1

- Size 3.25mm needles,

- Cast on 7
- Work 11 rows SS.
- Cast off.

To make up: Sew into a tube closing one end. Stuff with wool offcuts. Flatten and close end. Tie round tube tightly with a piece of yarn to form a head and torso.
Make arms and legs from i-cords. Attach.

DOLLY'S DRESS – MAKE TWO

- COLOUR 7
- Size 2mm needles

- Cast on 12
- K 2 rows
- 3rd row: Inc in next, P10, inc in last (14sts)
- Work 8 rows SS, starting with K
- 12th row: (K2tog) x 7 (7sts)
- Work 3 rows SS, starting with P
- Cast off

DOLLIE'S SLEEVE – MAKE TWO

- Cast on 7
- 1st row: P
- 2nd row: K2, inc in next, K1, inc in next, K2 (9sts)
- 3rd row: K
- 4th row: P2tog, P5, P2tog (7sts)
- 5th row: K2tog, K3, K2tog (5sts)
- 6th row: P2tog, P1, P2tog (3sts)
- Cast off

To make up: Steam press. Join front and back of dress on doll. Inset sleeves. Using 1.5mm crochet hook and COLOUR 4 crochet a frill at neck and hem of dress in single chain, catching it every few stitches to form a scalloped edging. Shoes are embroidered on using the same wool as the Bairn's shoes. Stitch on tiny beads for fastenings.
Add beads for eyes. The hair is a piece of the crinkled yarn used for the Bairn's hair. Finish by giving her an expression of your choice and hand over to the Bairn for a cuddle.

You will need

MATERIALS:

Colour Codes:
1 Rowan Baby Merino Silk DK
(Shade SH674 – Shell Pink) – For Body
2 Debbie Bliss Rialto 4ply
(Shade 22003 – Black) – For Boots
3 Sublime Baby Cashmerino silk DK
(Shade 0300 – Navy) – For Suit
4 Rowan Baby Merino Silk DK
(Shade SH682 – Deep) – For Bow Tie
5 Debbie Bliss Rialto Lace
(Shade 44002 – Pale Grey) – For Shirt
6 Rowan Fine Tweed
(Shade Dent 373 – Rust) – For Cap
7 Debbie Bliss Andes (Shade 370019 –
Pale Grey) – For Hair and Whiskers

Beads for jacket buttons, waistcoat and eyes
Small white beads for shirt front
Reel of grey sewing thread
Stuffing

NEEDLES:

Size 10/3.25mm
Size 11/3.00mm
Size 12/2.75mm
Size 12/2.75mm double-ended
Size 13/2.25mm
Crochet hook 3.5mm
Darning needle

Granpaw's got green fingers

Granpaw

Granpaw an' his whiskers,
wid mak' the family proud,
Daddy o' the bowling green,
the envy o' the crowd.
"Yes," he thinks, "of a' my hopes,
it really wid be fine,
Boolin' Champ o' Scotland,
at the age o' ninety-nine."

Granpaw Broon can be more trouble than all the children put together. Always on the look out for a free feed or getting his washing done, he may not live at Glebe Street but he might as well. Look out for his portrait on the wall in many of the strips reacting to the antics of the family. He likes clootie dumplin', a dram, granny sookers, the boolin', his allotment and gossiping with his cronies.

BODY

COLOUR 1

- Size 10/3.25mm needles

BODY – FRONT

- Cast on 16
- 1st row: K
- 2nd row: P
- 3rd row: K1, inc in next, K12, inc in next, K1 (18sts)
- Work 3 rows SS, starting with P
- 7th row: K1, K2tog, K2, K2tog, K4, K2tog, K2, K2tog, K1 (14sts)
- Work 3 rows SS, starting with P
- 11th row: K2, inc in next, K8, inc in next, K2 (16sts)
- 12th row: P
- 13th row: Inc in 1st, K3, inc in next, K6, inc in next, K3, inc in last (20sts)
- Work 5 rows SS, starting with P
- 19th row: K1, sl1, K1, psso, K14, K2tog, K1 (18sts)
- Work 3 rows SS, starting with P
- 23rd row: K1, sl1, K1, psso, K12, K2tog, K1 (16sts)
- 24th row: P1, P2tog, P10, P2tog, P1 (14sts)
- 25th row: K1, sl1, K1, psso, K8, K2tog, K1 (12sts)
- 26th row: P
- Cast off

BODY – BACK

- Cast on 16
- 1st row: K
- 2nd row: P
- 3rd row: K2, inc in next, K1, inc in next, K6, inc in next, K1, inc in next, K2 (20sts)
- 4th row: P

- 5th row: K3, inc in next, K1, inc in next, K8, inc in next, K1, inc in next, K3 (24sts)
- Work 3 rows SS, starting with P
- 9th row: K1, K2tog, K18, K2tog, K1 (22sts)
- 10th row: P
- 11th row: K2, K2tog, K1, K2tog, K8, K2tog, K1, K2tog, K2 (18sts)
- 12th row: P
- 13th row: (K2, K2tog)x4, K2 (14sts)
- Work 5 rows SS, starting with P
- 19th row: K1, inc in next, K4, inc in next, inc in next, K4, inc in next, K1 (18sts)
- Work 7 rows SS beginning with P
- 27th row: K1, sl1, K1, psso, K12, K2tog, K1 (16sts)
- 28th row: P1, P2tog, P10, P2tog, P1 (14sts)
- 29th row: K1, sl1, K1, psso, K8, K2tog, K1 (12sts)
- 30th row: P
- Cast off

To make up: Join front to back. Stuff.

ARMS – MAKE TWO

COLOUR 1

- Size 10/3.25mm needles

WORKING FROM SHOULDER TO WRIST

- Cast on 5
- 1st row: K
- 2nd row: P
- 3rd row: K row – inc in 1st and last (7sts)
- 4th row: P
- 5th row: K row – inc in 1st and last (9sts)
- Work 25 rows starting with P

TO CREATE LEFT HAND

- 31st row: K2, put 2 on pin, K5

- 32nd row: P to end bringing 2 sections together (7sts)
- 33rd row: K
- 34th row: P
- 35th row: K2tog, K2tog, K2tog, K1
- 36th row: P2tog, P2tog
- Pull thread through

TO CREATE RIGHT HAND

- 31st row: K5, put 2 on pin, K2 (7sts)
- 32nd row: P
- 33rd row: K
- 34th row: P
- 35th row: K1, K2tog, K2tog, K2tog
- 36th row: P2tog, P2tog
- Pull thread through

THUMB – SAME FOR BOTH HANDS

- Size 12/2.75mm double-ended needles
- Put 2sts from pin on double-ended needle
- Join thread, K2
- K2tog as i-cord
- Pull thread through

To make up: Join seams. Stuff.

BOOTS AND LEGS – MAKE TWO

COLOUR 2

- Size 10/3.25mm needles

- Cast on 20
- 1st row: K
- 2nd row: P
- 3rd row: K8, K2tog, K2tog, K8 (18sts)
- 4th row: P8, P2tog, P8 (17sts)
- 5th row: K

- 6th row: P
- 7th row: K4, cast off 9, K3 (8sts)
- 8th row: P, pulling 2 sections of 4sts together
- Work 4 rows SS, starting with K
- 13th row: K1, inc in next, K4, inc in next, K1 (10sts)
- 14th row: P
- Break wool, JOIN COLOUR 1
- Work 6 rows SS, starting with K
- 21st row: K1, inc in next, K6, inc in next, K1 (12sts)
- Work 22 rows SS, starting with P
- Cast off

To make up: Sew-up sole of boot – stuff boot. Join leg seam and stuff.

Tip: Stuff boots with offcuts of black wool rather than white wadding, which tends to show through.

HEAD

COLOUR 1
- Size 10/3.25mm needles

HEAD – BACK
- Cast on 6
- 1st row: K
- 2nd row: P
- 3rd row: K
- 4th row: P, inc in 1st and last (8sts)
- Work 2 rows SS, starting with K
- 7th row: K row, inc in 1st and last (10sts)
- 8th row: P
- 9th row: K3, inc in next, K2, inc in next, K3 (12sts)
- 10th row: P

- 11th row: K2, (inc in next)x3, K2, (inc in next)x3, K2 (18sts)
- Work 5 rows SS, starting with P
- 17th row: K1, sl1, K1, psso, K2, sl1, K1, psso, K4, K2tog, K2, K2tog, K1 (14sts)
- 18th row: P
- 19th row: K1, (sl1, K1, psso)x3, (K2tog)x3, K1 (8sts)
- 20th row: P
- Cast off

HEAD – FRONT (RIGHT SIDE)
- Cast on 5
- 1st row: K
- 2nd row: P
- 3rd row: Cast on 2, K to end (7sts)
- 4th row: P5, inc in next, inc in next (9sts)
- 5th row: K1, inc in next, inc in next, K6 (11sts)
- 6th row: P11 – break wool, leave sts on needle

HEAD – FRONT (LEFT SIDE)
- With WS facing cast on 5, turn – now working on these 5sts only:
- 1st row: K
- 2nd row: P
- 3rd row: K, cast on 2 (7sts)
- 4th row: P1, inc in next, inc in next, P4 (9sts)
- 5th row: K6, inc in next, inc in next, K1 (11sts)
- 6th row: P11
- 7th row: K across 2 pieces to join, K10, K2tog, K10 (21sts)
- 8th row: P1, P2tog, P15, P2tog, P1 (19sts)
- Work 4 rows SS, starting with K
- 13th row: K1, sl1, K1, psso, K13, K2tog, K1

- (17sts)
- 14th row: P
- 15th row: K1, sl1, K1, psso, K11, K2tog, K1 (15sts)
- 16th row: P
- 17th row: K1, sl1, K1, psso, K9, K2tog, K1 (13sts)
- 18th row: P1, P2tog, P7, P2tog, P1 (11sts)
- 19th row: K1, sl1, K1, psso, K5, K2tog, K1 (9sts)
- 20th row: P
- Cast off

To make up: Join seam under chin. Join front and back together. Stuff. Attach to body.

SHIRT

COLOUR 5
- Size 13/2.25mm needles

LEFT FRONT
- Cast on 14
- Work 21 rows SS, starting with K – Each P row starts with K2
- 22nd row: Cast off 3 P to end (11sts)
- 23rd row: K
- 24th row: Cast off 2, P to end (9sts)
- 25th row: Cast off 5, K to end (4sts)
- Cast off

RIGHT FRONT
- Cast on 14
- Work 20 rows SS, starting with K – Each P row ends with K2
- 21st row: Cast off 3, K to end (11sts)
- 22nd row: P
- 23rd row: Cast off 2, K to end (9sts)
- 24th row: Cast off 5, P to end (4sts)
- Cast off

To make up: Stitch onto body front at shoulders and hips. Add 3 to 4 small white beads for buttons.

COLLAR

COLOUR 5
- Size 13/2.25mm needles

- Cast on 28
- 1st row: K
- 2nd row: K1, P26, K1
- 3rd row: K
- 4th row: K1, P26, K1
- 5th row: K1, inc in next, K5, inc in next, K1, inc in next, K8, inc in next, K1, inc in next, K5, inc in next, K1 (34sts)
- 6th row: K1, P32, K1
- 7th row: K
- 8th row: K1, P32, K1
- 9th row: K row, inc in last
- Cast off

To make up: Fold and iron under a damp cloth. Attach around neck and to shirt front.

TROUSERS

COLOUR 3
- Size 11/3.00mm needles

RIGHT LEG
- Cast on 19
- Work 36 rows SS, starting with K
- 37th row: K9, inc in next, K9 (20sts)
- Work 7 rows SS, starting with P
- 45th row: Inc in 1st, K8, inc in next, K9, inc in last (23sts)
- 46th row: P
- 47th row: Cast off 2, K to end (21sts)

- 48th row: Cast off 2, P to end (19sts)
- Work 2 rows SS, starting with K
- Put on pin

LEFT LEG
- Cast on 19
- Work as right leg to row 50
- Knitting legs together, starting with left leg:
- 51st row: K2tog, K16, K last stitch of left leg with first stitch of right leg – K16, K2tog (33sts)
- Work 12 rows SS, starting with P
- Cast off

- To make up: Join inside leg seams. Join crotch. Dress doll.

WAISTCOAT

COLOUR 3
- Size 11/3.00mm needles

RIGHT FRONT
- Cast on 8
- 1st row: K2, turn –
- 2nd row: P1, inc in next (9sts)
- 3rd row: K1, inc in next, K4, turn – (10sts)
- 4th row: P6, inc in next (11sts)
- 5th row: K1, inc in next, K to end (12sts)
- 6th row: P11, K1
- 7th row: K
- 8th row: P11, K1
- 9th row: K
- 10th row: P11, K1
- 11th row: K
- 12th row: P11, K1
- 13th row: K10, inc in next, K1 (13sts)
- 14th row: P12, K1
- 15th row: K

- 16th row: P12, K1
- 17th row: K
- 18th row: P12, K1
- 19th row: K
- 20th row: Cast off 2, P9, K1 (11sts)
- 21st row: K9, K2tog (10sts)
- 22nd row: K1, P2tog, P6, K1 (9sts)
- 23rd row: K1, sl1, K1, psso, K to end (8sts)
- 24th row: K1, P4, P2tog, K1 (7sts)
- 25th row: K1, sl1, K1, psso, K to end (6sts)
- 26th row: K1, P4, K1
- 27th row: K1, sl1, K1, psso, K to end (5sts)
- 28th row: K1, P3, K1
- 29th row: K1, sl1, K1, psso, K to end (4sts)
- 30th row: K1, P2, K1
- 31st row: K1, sl1, K1, psso, K to end (3sts)
- Cast off

LEFT FRONT
- Cast on 8
- 1st row: P2, turn –
- 2nd row: K1, inc in next (9sts)
- 3rd row: Inc in 1st, P5, turn – (10sts)
- 4th row: K5, inc in next, K1 (11sts)
- 5th row: Inc in 1st, P to end (12sts)
- 6th row: K
- 7th row: K1, P to end
- 8th row: K
- 9th row: K1, P to end
- 10th row: K
- 11th row: K1, P to end
- 12th row: K
- 13th row: K1, P to end
- 14th row: K1, inc in next, K to end (13sts)
- 15th row: K1, P to end
- 16th row: K
- 17th row: K1, P to end
- 18th row: K

- 19th row: K1, P to end
- 20th row: Cast off 2, K to end (11sts)
- 21st row: K1, P8, P2tog (10sts)
- 22nd row: K2tog, K to end (9sts)
- 23rd row: K1, P2tog, P5, K1 (8sts)
- 24th row: K5, K2tog, K1 (7sts)
- 25th row: K1, P2tog, P3, K1 (6sts)
- 26th row: K
- 27th row: K1, P2tog, P2, K1 (5sts)
- 28th row: K
- 29th row: K1, P2tog, P1, K1 (4sts)
- 30th row: K
- 31st row: K1, P2tog, K1 (3sts)
- 32nd row: K
- Cast off

To make up: Join to front of doll. Dress doll. Add beads for buttons at centre front.

JACKET

COLOUR 3
- Size 11/3.00mm needles

FRONT AND BACK – LEFT
- Cast on 24
- Work 10 rows SS, starting with K
- 11th row: K11, K2tog, K11 (23sts)
- 12th row: P
- Set aside on pin

FRONT AND BACK – RIGHT
- Cast on 26
- Work 10 rows SS, starting with K
- 11th row: K11, K2tog, K13 (25sts)
- 12th row: Cast off 2, P to end (23sts)

TO JOIN JACKET PIECES TOGETHER
- With RS facing work row 13 across front and back right, followed by front and back left
- 13th row: K22, K last stitch from right side and first from left side together, K22 (45sts)
- Work 3 rows SS, starting with P
- 17th row: K13, K2tog, K15, K2tog, K13 (43sts)
- Work 3 rows SS, starting with P
- 21st row: K13, inc in next, K15, inc in next, K13 (45sts)
- 22nd row: P
- 23rd row: K11, inc in next, K21, inc in next, K11 (47sts)
- 24th row: P
- 25th row: K1, inc in next, K43, inc in next, K1 (49sts)
- 26th row: K2, P45, K2
- 27th row: P2, K45, P2
- 28th row: K3, P10, cast off 2, P18, cast off 2, P9, K3 (45sts)

WORKING ON RIGHT FRONT (13STS)
- 29th row: P3, K8, K2tog (12sts)
- 30th row: P9, K3
- 31st row: P4, K8
- 32nd row: P8, K4
- 33rd row: P4, K8
- 34th row: P7, K5
- 35th row: P5, K7
- 36th row: P2tog, P5, K5 (11sts)
- 37th row: Cast off 3, P1, K6 (8sts)
- 38th row: P6, put last 2 sts on pin for collar, turn –
- 39th row: K6
- 40th row: Cast off 3, P2 (3sts)
- Cast off

WORKING ON JACKET BACK – NEXT 19 STS – RS FACING
- Work 7 rows SS, starting with K
- 36th row: P2tog, P15, P2tog (17sts)
- 37th row: K
- 38th row: P
- 39th row: Cast off 3, K13 (14sts)
- 40th row: Cast off 3, P10 (11sts)
- 41st row: Cast off 2, K8 (9sts)
- 42nd row: Cast off 2, put remaining 7 sts on pin for collar

WORKING ON FRONT LEFT – REMAINING 13 STS – RS FACING
- 29th row: K2tog, K8, P3 (12sts)
- 30th row: K3, P9
- 31st row: K8, P4
- 32nd row: K4, P8
- 33rd row: K8, P4
- 34th row: K5, P7
- 35th row: K7, P5
- 36th row: K5, P5, P2tog (11sts)
- 37th row: K6, P5
- 38th row: Cast off 3, K1, P6 (8sts)
- 39th row: K6, put last 2 sts on pin for collar, turn –
- 40th row: P6
- 41st row: K6
- 42nd row: P6
- 43rd row: Cast off 3, K2 (3sts)
- Cast off

To make up: Join shoulder seams. Catch top of centre back vent.

UPPER COLLAR

- Size 12/2.75mm needles

- Working with WS facing
- 1st row: K2 sts from left lapel, pick up 6 sts along left front neck, K7 from back neck, pick up 6 sts along right front neck, K2 sts from right lapel (23sts)
- 2nd row: P
- 3rd row: K
- 4th row: Inc in 1st, P20, inc in next, K1 (25sts)
- 5th row: K9, inc in next, K5, inc in next, K8, inc in last (28sts)
- Cast off loosely

To make up: Steam press to tidy collar and lapels.

JACKET SLEEVES – MAKE TWO

- Cast on 14
- Work 10 rows SS, starting with K
- 11th row: K row, inc in 1st and last st (16sts)
- Work 5 rows SS, starting with P
- 17th row: For left sleeve, K3, inc in next, K12 (17sts) For right sleeve, K11, inc in next, K4 (17sts)
- Work 8 rows SS, starting with P
- 26th row: Cast off 2, P to end (15sts)
- 27th row: Cast off 2, K to end (13sts)
- 28th row: P2tog, P9, P2tog (11sts)
- Work 3 rows SS, starting with K
- 32nd row: P2tog, P7, P2tog (9sts)
- 33rd row: K2tog, K5, K2tog (7sts)
- Cast off

To make up: Join seams. Inset to jacket. To finish the suit dress doll and add beads as front and cuff buttons.

CAP

COLOUR 6

- Size 12/2.75mm
- Size 12/2.75mm double-ended

CROWN – USE 12/2.75MM DOUBLE-ENDED

- Cast on 36
- Work 3 rows GS
- Join into circle
- 1st round: (inc in next, inc in next, K1) x12 (60sts)
- Work 6 rounds in K
- 8th round: (K2tog, K2tog, K1) x12 (36sts)
- Work 4 rounds in K
- 13th round: (K2togx4, K1) x4 (20sts)
- Work 4 rounds in K
- 18th round: K2tog to end (10sts)
- 19th round: K2tog to end (5sts)
- Pull wool through all stitches

BRIM – USE 12/2.75MM

- Cast on 19
- 1st row: K19
- 2nd row: P18, turn –
- 3rd row: K17, turn –
- 4th row: P16, turn –
- 5th row: K15, turn –
- 6th row: P14, turn –
- 7th row: K13, turn –
- 8th row: P12, turn –
- 9th row: K11, turn –
- 10th row: P11, turn –
- 11th row: K12, turn –
- 12th row: P14, turn –
- 13th row: K16, turn –
- 14th row: P18
- Cast off

To make up: Stitch up garter stitch rows for cap band. Fold brim in half, joining cast on and cast off edges together and sew onto underside of crown.
Stuff crown with wadding and steam to shape. Remove wadding.

BOW-TIE

COLOUR 4

- Size 13/2.25mm needles

- Cast on 3
- 1st row: K
- 2nd row: P
- 3rd row: Inc in 1st, K1, inc in last (5sts)
- Work 34 rows in SS, starting with P
- 38th row: P2tog, P1, P2tog (3sts)
- Work 8 rows SS, starting with K
- Cast off

To make up: Fold into a bow and stitch. Wind narrow end round at the centre of bow and secure with a few stitches.
Slip onto a length of yarn at the centre point and add to doll, tucking yarn under the collar. Secure and fasten off at centre back of neck

HAIR, BEARD AND WHISKERS

COLOUR 7

- COLOUR 7
- 3.25mm needles

Tip: It is easier to fit the hair, beard and whiskers after the nose and ears have been placed and attached: See TO CREATE FACE.

HAIR

- Cast on 13
- 1st row: K
- 2nd row: P
- 3rd row: Inc in 1st, K11, inc in last (15sts)
- 4th row: P
- 5th row: Inc in 1st, K13, inc in last (17sts)
- Cast off loosely

To make up: Fit to head. Stitch in place.

BEARD

- Cast on 16
- 1st row: K
- 2nd row: P15 turn –
- 3rd row: K14 turn –
- 4th row: P13 turn –
- 5th row: K12 turn –
- 6th row: P11 turn –
- 7th row: K12 turn –
- 8th row: P13 turn –
- 9th row: K14 turn –
- 10th row: P15 turn –
- Cast off

To make up: Sew the cast-off edge around the face to form the underside of the beard. Fold up around chin, pin to shape and stitch in place. Use a darning needle to stitch loops of yarn to the beard to shape.

WHISKERS

Fold a length of yarn over on itself 4 or 5 times to form a small skein 4-5cm in length. Secure at the centre and attach to face. Curve to shape (dampen fingers and tweak – allow to dry) and using sewing thread, stitch and shape loops together on both sides to form moustache.

TO CREATE FACE

Refer to a cartoon to get the flavour of Granpaw. Add beads for eyes. The nose is fashioned from a crocheted chain of flesh coloured wool – be generous. The ears are fashioned from a crocheted chain curled around on itself and stitched together. Add brows in COLOUR 7.

Glossary

4 Ply – thickness of wool

DK – abbreviation for 'double knitting' (thickness of wool)

GS – abbreviation for 'garter stitch'; knit every row

i-cord – a process for knitting a tube or stalk or stem; with double-ended needles knit a row, slide the stitches to the other end of the needle (do not turn the knitting) knit the next row, pulling the yarn tight on the first stitch, so that the knitting forms a tube, continue in this way until cord is desired length

inc – increase by knitting into the front and the back of the stitch

1 and 1 rib – K1, P1

K – abbreviation for 'knit'

K2tog – abbreviation for 'knit 2 stitches together'

P – abbreviation for 'purl'

P2tog – abbreviation for 'purl 2 stitches together'

psso – abbreviation for 'pass slip stitch over'; pass the slip stitch over the next stitch

Reverse SS – the same process as SS but the knobbly side is to the right side

RS – abbreviation for 'the right side of the work'

SS – abbreviation for 'stocking stitch'; alternate knit and purl rows, creating a smooth finish on one side, usually the right side

ssk – slip two stitches one at a time onto the right needle then knit them together

sl – abbreviation for 'slip'; slip the stitch onto the right needle without either knitting or purling

st(s) – abbreviation for 'stitch' or 'stitches' if more than one

WS – abbreviation for 'the wrong side of the work'

yf – the abbreviation of 'yarn forward'; bring the yarn over the needle before working the next stitch

yo – abbreviation for 'yarn over'; bring the yarn over the needle before working the next stitch

Hints and Tips

- The wools used in the patterns are listed; however, because we are working fairly small-scale you may choose to replace any suggested yarns with oddments you already have. Check that your yarn is of a similar weight/ply.

- All ends of wool should be finished off by weaving in before making up.

- Joining seams: To give a firm finish to seams, join using original weight of yarn, or for a softer finish and with very small pieces, pare yarn down.

- Pressing of knitted pieces: Generally these small items benefit from a gentle steam press before making up. If you want to check the finish, knit a small square and test-press before starting one of the patterns.

- For a better fit: As every knitter works with a different tension you may wish to work up or down a size of needle.

- Stuffing heads & limbs: Try not to over- or under-stuff. Bear in mind the finished character, and his or her shape.

- Heads & faces can be made more characterful by careful stuffing. To further define or alter a face shape, run a darning needle threaded with yarn through from one side to the other, pull gently and fasten off. Work from an image if possible, and look at shape of head – front, back and side views. Is there any feature that is particularly prominent? Using smaller amounts of stuffing at a time will give you more sensitive shaping.